FOLLOWING JESUS

Perspectives from Twelve Christian Traditions

HAROLD HEIE AND JOHN G. STACKHOUSE, JR.
Foreword by Richard J. Mouw

Contributors

David Ford

Christina Wassell

Mark Ellingsen

Michael J. King

Randall Balmer

Wesley Granberg-Michaelson

David Gushee

Christopher Gehrz

Sarah Lancaster

Farris Blount

Robert Millet

J. Terry Todd

Dedicated to those followers of Jesus who exemplify that rare combination of holding to the beliefs of their Christian tradition with deep conviction while also loving those from other traditions who disagree with them by creating safe and welcoming spaces to express and talk respectfully about their disagreements for the purpose of learning from one another.

2024 First Printing

Following Jesus: Perspectives from Twelve Christian Traditions

Copyright © 2024 by Harold Heie and John G. Stackhouse, Jr.

ISBN: 979-8-218-96814-4

10 9 8 7 6 5 4 3 2 1

All rights reserved. No portion of this book may be reproduced, stored in an electronic retrieval system, or transmitted in any form or by any means—electronic, mechanical, photocopy, recording, or any other—except for brief quotations in printed reviews, without the prior permission of the copyright holder.

Published by Harold Heie and John G. Stackhouse, Jr.
Orange City, Iowa

Printed in the United States of America

Foreword
Richard J. Mouw

During the weeks when we were celebrating the 500-year anniversary of the Protestant Reformation, I participated in a public dialogue with a Catholic theologian. He was a good friend, and we got along well as we addressed some of the big issues that we Protestants have long debated with Catholics: justification by faith, sacraments, Marian doctrine, prayers to the saints, and so on.

When we turned things over to our audience for Q and A, a young woman stood to thank us for the friendly tone of our dialogue. But she also confessed her impatience with the subject matter of the evening. "Why can't we just concentrate on the topic where there can be no disagreement—How we can just follow Jesus together?"

My Catholic dialogue partner said she was raising a helpful concern, and I echoed his commendation. Then together we mentioned a few areas where our two communities should be working together in service to Jesus. I did not want to pursue the subject more at that point, but I am not convinced that "there can be no disagreement" about what it means to follow Jesus.

I thought about her plea as I read about the conversations reported in this fine book, and I was reinforced in my sense that there is plenty to discuss on the subject of following Jesus. I was raised in an evangelical environment where following Jesus meant talking to others about accepting Jesus as their Savior so that they too could be "saved to tell others." Some Catholic friends in my youth gave the impression that following Jesus meant coming to school with the cross on their foreheads on Ash Wednesday and then "giving something up for Lent." Later I met Mennonites who were committed to living out what Jesus taught in the Sermon on the Mount—a part of the Gospels that I did not hear much about in my Reformed church!

Again, the impression that work is required to arrive at a consensus about following Jesus has been confirmed for me by this book. But the conversations that we learn about here also give us hope. One reason for the hope is a very specific one: The convenor of these conversations is Harold Heie. Here again Harold has taken it on as his calling to show that we can get beyond serious disagreements by sticking with each other in keeping the conversation going. He has taught many of us the how and why of serious sustained *listening* to each other.

As I have observed Harold's devotion to promoting the cultivation of listening skills over the years of our friendship, it is clear to me that *empathy* is at the heart of what he is about. Empathy is my experiencing the feelings and concerns of others as if they were my own. To be sure, attempting to understand the views of, say, a self-professed atheist, from the "inside," as it were, can be a special challenge for a Christian. But it is an important challenge, and the challenge is not lessened when we are engaging fellow Christians on matters where we disagree.

We Christians do have access to spiritual resources to draw upon, though, in engaging in the more difficult challenges with empathy. Simone Weil put it bluntly: The humble awareness of our own sin can lead us, she said, "to contemplate our stupidity." We are indeed sinners, deeply affected by our fallenness. And to top it off, we are finite creatures. Even in our most noble efforts to grasp the truth, we fall far short of omniscience.

An awareness of this combination of our sinfulness and our finitude should cultivate in us a desire to learn from others. When we pray—as we should frequently—the "Search me, O God" prayer of Psalm 139, we should expect that the Lord will use other persons as appointees to his search party.

God continues to deputize Harold Heie as an important search party organizer. And this time around, Harold has put together a marvelously diverse search party of Christians who have been cultivating listening skills. This book brings hope that in the midst of our divisive times, it can be done: There are Christians who are willing to engage each other on matters where they disagree—even on the all-important topic of what it means to follow Jesus!

Acknowledgments

I first express my deepest gratitude to the highly regarded representatives of twelve Christian traditions who graciously agreed to be conversation partners (CPs) for the electronic conversation (eCircle) on my website, respectfulconversation.net, that led to this book. I was not able to offer them a penny of remuneration for their work. Nevertheless, they shared my commitment to respectfully engaging those with whom they had disagreements and my desire to bridge divisive lines across Christian traditions about what it means to "follow Jesus." This led them to faithfully post very thoughtful and, at times, provocative responses to the Leading Questions that I posed throughout our year of electronic conversation. I cannot find adequate words to thank them for their marvelous contributions.

I give a special word of appreciation to my Anglican CP, Randall Balmer from Dartmouth College, who served as my Project Consultant. He gave me sage advice as I was shaping this ecumenical conversation. Randall has also been a supporter of various initiatives in my Respectful Conversation Project, sending me words of encouragement, for which I am most appreciative. I was especially encouraged when he sent me an email at the end of this ecumenical conversation in which he asserted, "This year-long conversation has been a smashing success."

I want to thank Richard Mouw for writing a generous foreword for this book. I have been standing on Richard's shoulders for the past decade or so, since he has been a pioneer in orchestrating respectful conversations about contentious issues. His past work that has been particularly relevant to this book was his extended evangelical/Mormon dialogue with Robert Millet, his Mormon friend, who served so well as my Latter-day Saint CP. It is an honor and source of great encouragement to have a Christian statesman of Richard's stature and sterling reputation express appreciation for this book.

I want to thank my Canadian friend John Stackhouse for writing a splendid concluding grand synthesis essay for this book. John and I go back to the late 1980s, when I hired him to teach history at Northwestern College in Iowa. After a few good years together at NWC, we both went our separate ways. But in our years working together, I came to appreciate John's creativity and his willingness to think outside the box. I am thankful for the way in which John demonstrated so well both of these abilities in his concluding essay for this book.

I also want to thank Mark Noll and George Marsden for their splendid endorsements of this book. I am honored that these two highly regarded Christian scholars strongly recommended its content to potential readers.

I thank Dan Hefferan from the Dauntless Digital Company, who served so exceptionally well as my website manager for

ACKNOWLEDGEMENTS

the electronic conversation that led to this book. Since I am not very Internet savvy, I was dependent on Dan's invaluable assistance, without which this book would not have come to fruition.

This self-published book was made possible because of the marvelous help provided by Paraclete Press, with excellent work accomplished by Paul Tingley, Michael Hale, and Sarah Kanaga.

Paraclete Press is the publishing house of a Cape Cod Benedictine community. They are located in Orleans, Massachusetts (on Cape Cod).

The invaluable assistance provided by Paul, Mike and Sarah included internal text formatting, the design of the front and back covers, and arranging for posting on Amazon. Throughout this process, they exhibited great patience and attention to all the intricacies of self-publishing. I cannot find adequate words to express my deep appreciation. Thank you! If any reader of this book is interested in self-publishing a book, I highly recommend that you first contact Paul Tingley at Paraclete Press (pault@paracletepress.com).

Finally, I wish to especially thank my wife, Pat, for her significant role in making this book possible. You will not fully appreciate the magnitude of Pat's contribution without my sharing a personal account of the challenging circumstances under which this entire project was carried out: In October of 2020, I was diagnosed with cancer. Thankfully, a successful regimen of radiation and chemotherapy eliminated this cancer. But in April of 2022, I learned that my cancer had migrated to another part of my body and, as I write these words (in August 2022), I am in the midst of chemo treatments for this cancer.

FOLLOWING JESUS

In light of this timeline, the twelve-month ecumenical conversation that I hosted on my website, which started on August 1, 2021, and my subsequent writing of this book were all carried out while I was being treated for cancer. Some friends of mine have wondered how I could carry out these demanding tasks while suffering from and being treated for cancer. Let me provide an explanation, which will set the context for my special tribute to my wife, Pat.

Two things that I love to do are writing and synthesizing scholarly work—trying to make coherent sense out of seemingly conflicting perspectives on contentious issues. This project has provided me with the opportunity to pursue these two loves. Although I have experienced the mysteries of God's presence with me in the midst of my struggles with cancer, for which I am very thankful, I also needed something to keep my mind off my health struggles. The ability to spend significant time each day immersed in my two loves has met this need, providing a therapeutic distraction.

Enter Pat Heie. As you can imagine, I have needed a significant amount of home care since October of 2020. The vast majority of this home care has been provided by Pat, who has worked tirelessly to care for my special needs as a cancer patient who still wants to pursue his two loves. So, my entire ecumenical conversation and this resulting book would not have happened without Pat's marvelous care for me. No words will suffice for me to express the depth of my appreciation to my beloved Pat for this marvelous gift.

Contents

Foreword by Richard Mouw 1

Acknowledgments 5

Introduction: Learning from Others about What 11
It Means to Follow Jesus, Harold Heie

I. The Orthodox Tradition, David Ford 19

II. The Roman Catholic Tradition, Christina Wassell 29

III. The Lutheran Tradition, Mark Ellingsen 43

IV. The Anabaptist Tradition, Michael King 61

V. The Anglican Tradition, Randall Balmer 79

VI. The Reformed Tradition, ... 95
Wesley Granberg-Michaelson

VII. The Baptist Tradition, David Gushee 109

VIII. The Pietist Tradition, Christopher Gehrz 121

IX. The Wesleyan Tradition, Sarah Lancaster 137

X. The Black Church Tradition, Farris Blount 151

XI. The Latter-day Saints Tradition, Robert Millet 165

XII. The Pentecostal Tradition, J. Terry Todd 177

XIII. Diversity and Blessing, John G. Stackhouse Jr. 195

Conclusion: What I Have Learned from 219
   Our Conversation, Harold Heie

About the Authors 227

Contributors 231

Introduction
Harold Heie

Learning from Others about What It Means to Follow Jesus

Christians disagree about many contentious issues. Passionate debates about human sexuality and political affiliation are but two examples. But in the midst of these disagreements, I believe that one truth all who profess Christ agree on is that to be a Christian includes an aspiration to follow Jesus. This belief is an underlying premise for this book, based on the biblical teaching that God desires for those who profess to be Christians be transformed into the "likeness of Christ" (2 Corinthians 3:18; 5:17).

But given this agreement, there are enormous disagreements across Christian traditions as to exactly what it means to follow Jesus. How have Christians responded to this multiplicity of beliefs about what it means to follow Jesus? Some have viewed this multiplicity to be tragic—a splintering of the singular vision for the visible Church inaugurated by Jesus.

Others have viewed this "manyness" to be a gift, believing that each Christian tradition can contribute to a fuller understanding of what it means to follow Jesus.

Both views are presented in this book, but the latter view is most prominent.

The Purposes of This Book

A. To report on the reflections of highly regarded representatives of twelve Christian traditions regarding the meaning(s) that their respective traditions give to the aspiration to follow Jesus.

B. To provide a much-needed resource toward the goal of "continuing the conversation" by posing questions that were raised and unanswered in these initial reports.

It is vitally important to emphasize that the second purpose of this book stems from my belief that the impact of this book would be severely limited if it only contained reports on the initial conversations among my twelve conversation partners (CPs). These initial conversations should be viewed as only the "beginnings" of what will hopefully be a series of "ongoing conversations" within and across our twelve traditions.

The Genesis of This Book

This book emerged from a twelve-month electronic conversation (eCircle) I hosted on my website, respectfulconversation.net, from August 2021 through July 2022. Titled "Following Jesus: Perspectives From Diverse Christian Traditions," this eCircle featured the postings of the twelve CPs listed below, who represent twelve different traditions that self-identify as

INTRODUCTION

"Christian." Dr. Randall Balmer, John Phillips Professor in Religion at Dartmouth College, served as my Project Consultant. The ordering of these twelve traditions is chronological, from oldest to newest, according to the generally accepted origination date of each tradition.

> August 2021: Orthodox – Dr. David Ford, Professor of Church History, St. Tikhon's Orthodox Theological Seminary
>
> September 2021: Roman Catholic – Ms. Christina Wassell, Catholic layperson who serves as a K–12 tutor and whose pilgrimage has taken her from immersion in two Protestant traditions to Catholicism
>
> October 2021: Lutheran – Dr. Mark Ellingsen, Professor of Church History, Interdenominational Theological Center, Atlanta
>
> November 2021: Anabaptist – Dr Michael J. King, President, Cascade Publishing House and former Academic Dean at Eastern Mennonite Seminary
>
> December 2021: Anglican – Dr. Randall Balmer, John Phillips Professor in Religion at Dartmouth College
>
> January 2022: Reformed – Dr. Wesley Granberg-Michaelson, Emeritus General Secretary, Reformed Church in America
>
> February 2022: Baptist – Dr. David Gushee, Professor of Christian Ethics and Director of the Center for Theology and Public Life, Mercer University
>
> March 2022: Pietist – Dr. Christopher Gehrz, History Department Chair, Bethel University (MN)

April 2022: Wesleyan – Dr. Sarah Lancaster, Professor in the Werner Chair in Theology, Methodist Theological School in Ohio

May 2022: The Black Church – Mr. Farris Blount, PhD candidate in Practical Theology, Boston University

June 2022: Latter-day Saints – Dr. Robert Millet, Professor Emeritus of Religious Education, Brigham Young University

July 2022: Pentecostal – Dr. J. Terry Todd, Associate Professor of American Religious Studies, Drew University

Each chapter 1-12 has four sections. The first section is the article posted on the first of each month by the CP representing the given tradition in response to the following Leading Question:

> What are the various views of those who worship in your tradition as to what it means to follow Jesus, and what is the primary view?

The second section for each chapter is my presentation of what I consider to be the "highlights" of the middle-of-the-month postings by the eleven other CPs in response to the following Leading Question:

> What major agreements and disagreements do you have with the views expressed in the first-of-the-month posting about what it means to follow Jesus, and what have you learned from that posting that has the potential to enrich, or possibly provide a corrective, to the primary view of those who seek to follow Jesus in your tradition?

The third section consists of my presentation of "Questions

for Future Conversations," which are posed to encourage readers to continue talking about the agreements and disagreements that are raised in this book (based on my hope that this book will be just the "beginning" of a series of conversations rather than both the beginning and the end).

The fourth section consists of a final end-of-the-month reflection from the CP for the tradition being featured in response to the following Leading Question:

> As you review the eleven middle-of-the-month postings from the other CPs, what were the main things you learned that that will be helpful to those who seek to faithfully follow Jesus in the future in your tradition?

Chapter 13 of this book, written by John Stackhouse, Professor of Religious Studies at Crandall University in Moncton, New Brunswick, is his attempt to create a grand synthesis of chapters 1–12 as an answer to the question "Where do we as Christians go from here?"

The book concludes with my essay on the topic "What I Have Learned from Our Conversation."

Two Caveats

In my enumeration of the "highlights" of the middle-of-the-month responses to the first-of-the-month posting of the CP representing the Christian tradition for the month, I had to "pick-and choose" from the rich diversity of reflections from the eleven other CPs.

As a result of this methodology, there were many invaluable insights presented in the online middle-of-the-month conversations from my other CPs that are not referenced in what I considered to be "highlights." Therefore, I apologize in advance to any CP who comes away from reading any given chapter with the feeling that I should have included insights from his or her middle-of the-month posting in my enumeration of "highlights."

A reader of this book will also notice that from time to time I inserted some personal beliefs about what it means to follow Jesus that have emerged from my Christian pilgrimage, which includes extensive immersion in three of the traditions being considered in this ecumenical conversation: the Pietist (of the Lutheran variety), the Reformed, and the Anabaptist. Therefore, while I seek to adequately report the highlights of the CPs' postings in a fair-minded manner, I also reveal some of my own beliefs about the issues being discussed, including some recommendations. I will certainly understand criticisms that I have not struck this balance well.

What the eCircle and This Book Hope to Model

An underlying assumption for the eCircle that led to this book is that Christians embedded in different Christian traditions who have significantly different beliefs about what it means to follow Jesus wish to learn from one another. In our day and age, that may win the gold medal for wishful thinking. Therefore, I conclude this introductory chapter with reflections on why the idea of learning from someone who disagrees with you is increasingly unheard of in American culture and how my eCircle and this book have taken bold steps to model learning from those with whom you have strong disagreements.

The root problem is the tribalism that is so rampant in our society—an us-versus-them mentality that says "me and my peo-

INTRODUCTION

ple" (like those who worship in my Christian tradition) have the whole truth about the issue at hand (like what it means to follow Jesus) and "those other folks" (like those who worship in other Christian traditions) have no truth to offer and, therefore, we have nothing to learn from them by respectfully talking about our disagreements.

Bold steps are required to overcome this tribalism. In the eCircle that led to this book, my boldest step (of three steps in a "Methodology" that I will propose in my concluding chapter in this book) was that my invitation to serve as a conversation partner in this ecumenical conversation included the expectation that all who expressed an interest in participating had to agree up-front to abide by the following set of five "Guidelines for Respectful Conversation" throughout the conversation:

1. I will try to listen well, providing each person with a welcoming space to express her beliefs about the questions that are posed.

2. I will seek to empathetically understand the reasons another person has for her beliefs about the questions that are posed.

3. I will express my beliefs about the questions that are posed and my reasons for holding those beliefs with clarity and conviction, but with a noncoercive style that invites conversation with a person who disagrees with me.

4. In my conversation with a person who disagrees with me about answers to the questions posed, I will explore whether we can find some common ground by critically examining my own beliefs in light of her contrary beliefs and the reasons she has for her beliefs.

5. Guided by the underlying values of humility, courage, patience, and love, when we cannot find common ground, I will always engage the person who disagrees with me in a way that demonstrates respect and concern for her wellbeing and does not foreclose the possibility of future conversations.

It is important to note the demands of the fourth guideline above. It requires going beyond the politeness that simply lets the other person speak without interruption, with no intention of re-examining my own beliefs in light of the contrary beliefs of the other, which is "weak listening." Rather, this guideline calls for "strong listening" where I commit to re-examining my own beliefs in light of what I have heard the other person say. My own hard-earned experience in moderating small-group conversation about contentious issues is that many conversation partners will exhibit politeness, which is good as far as it goes, but will not take the demanding leap into strong listening. Readers of my eCircle will be able to verify that my conversation partners modeled such strong listening to an admirable degree.

The foundational premise underlying this expectation for my conversation partners is that *to create a safe and welcoming space for someone who disagrees with me to express that disagreement and to then talk respectfully about that disagreement is a deep expression of love.* Another truth that all Christians can agree on is that Jesus called all those who profess to be his followers to love others.

I. The Orthodox Tradition
David Ford

What it Means to Follow Jesus

Due to space limitations, I can only offer here a glimpse into the profound and boundless glory of what it means to follow Jesus in the Orthodox tradition—a path of belief and practice that's been followed with remarkable consistency by millions of Orthodox Christians through twenty centuries. The spirituality, doctrines, liturgical life, and the conciliar/hierarchical structure of the Orthodox Church have remained unchanged at their core, beginning in the Apostolic age, with more "rings" of amplification and enrichment being added to the same "tree" through the centuries.

So in the Orthodox understanding, the way to follow Jesus that's been faithfully passed down to us is a truly time-tested, proven path. More importantly, it's a path that's God-inspired and God-directed, confirmed through the prayer—and all the spiritual experience—of countless people of every social, political, and economic background in every era, in a great number of cultures. Yet within the guidelines provided by the Orthodox tradition for how to follow Jesus, there is flexibility for each person to do so uniquely, depending upon one's unique needs and abilities.

Christians who are recognized as premier examples of this way of life are the Virgin Mary and the saints—those men, women, and children who most faithfully, fervently, and fully lived in vibrant communion with our Lord, God, and Savior Jesus Christ, many of whom gave their lives for him in martyrdom. Numerous saints are commemorated in the Orthodox Church every day of the year—the day we particularly honor them, asking for their prayers and being inspired by the holiness and fruitfulness of their lives.

Of course, not every Orthodox Christian follows Jesus with the same degree of faithfulness, fervency, holiness, and fruitfulness as the canonized saints have done. But there is, nevertheless, one basic way of following him that is the ideal, the hope and expectation for every Orthodox Christian—the path of aspiring to live in ever-closer, direct communion with him; being filled with his love, joy (John 15:11), and peace (John 14:27); striving to live in purity of thought, word, and deed; and ever trusting in his limitless mercy in anticipation of his second coming (Rev. 22:20), the resurrection of the dead, the last judgment, and eternal life in heaven, our true home (Phil. 3:20-21; cf. Phil. 3:7-14).

For this endeavor, the Orthodox Church provides many resources for spiritual growth, including daily study of the Holy Scriptures, being guided by the church's long-standing interpretation of them; time-honored prayers for many occasions; rich liturgical life, replete with psalmody and including hymns filled with devotion and sound doctrine; the sacraments—especially the Eucharist, celebrated at every Divine Liturgy, and the Sacrament of Confession; celebration of the many great holy days (Feasts) of the church year; the writings of the church fathers; the lives of the saints; the doctrinal proclamations and canons of the ecumenical councils—especially the Nicene Creed; veneration of the holy icons; the sign of the cross; the connection with one's patron saint and guardian angel; and the spiritual direction of one's spiritual father.

Even the great numbers of monastics through the centuries, who have, generally speaking, most entirely given their lives to following Jesus in direct service to him and his church, do not follow him in a way that's substantially different from how everyone else follows him in our tradition—except that, most likely, they pray, fast, and attend services more and live more simply than the rest of us! And, of course, they live in sexual abstinence, while the married enjoy their God-given marital relations. But in both cases, we're called to live in sexual purity—total abstinence for the monastics, and total faithfulness to one's spouse for the married (with marriage understood as between one man and one woman, mirroring Christ the bridegroom's love for his bride, the Church—Eph. 5:23-32).

To say a bit more about particular features of the Orthodox way of following Jesus:

Worshiping him "in spirit and in truth" (John 4:24)—participating regularly in the prayer-filled and Scripture-filled liturgical/sacramental life of the church; entering with humility and awe into the majesty and beauty of the communal worship of God in church services; participating in the alternating rhythms of feasting and fasting according to the patterns designated in the church year.

FOLLOWING JESUS

Being in vibrant communion/fellowship with his saints—the living, the departed, and in a very special way, the glorified (those canonized by the church as saints): "God is wondrous in his saints" (Ps. 67:36, Septuagint); "I believe in . . . the communion of saints" (the Apostles' Creed); "surrounded by so great a cloud of witnesses" (Heb. 12:1; Heb. 12:23); being surrounded by the saints in their grace-bearing icons ("windows to heaven") in church and at home (particularly in the icon corner); asking for their prayers; reading their lives and their writings.

Endeavoring to live without sin in thought, word, and deed, in purity in mind, soul, and body, including sexual purity (Matt. 5:48, Heb. 12:14, 1 Thess. 4:3, 1 Peter 1:15-16, Lev. 11:44-45). Growing in communion with Jesus is accomplished in large measure through keeping his commandments (John 15:10; also 15:14 and 14:15). And we remember that avoiding sin requires careful attentiveness to the voice of our conscience, ongoing ascetical effort to control and properly direct our passions, and repenting for our sins. We endeavor to be watchful over our thoughts and feelings, trying to be quick in rejecting deleterious thoughts and feelings (called *logismoi*) that disrupt our relationship with Jesus.

Endeavoring to surrender our own will to his will (Luke 22:42); this includes surrendering our own will appropriately as we self-sacrificially serve others, placing their needs and desires ahead of our own.

Endeavoring to maintain our trust in Christ no matter what happens—no matter what cross he may ask us to bear in terms of personal hardships and the hardships of those close to us (Matt. 16:24; Luke 9:23). We offer our hardships, sufferings, and sorrows to him, linking them with his suffering on the cross, knowing that he often allows them as a means for us to grow in faith and trust in him, and for us to grow in virtue (James 1:2-4, Romans 5:3-4, 1 Peter 1:6-9). Yet we also pray to Christ for deliverance from afflictions, mindful that miracles often happen, but always concluding with asking that his will be done.

Endeavoring to maintain a regular rule of prayer, developed and sustained, ideally, under the guidance of a spiritual father/director (often the priest of one's parish), before whom one confesses one's sins to God regularly in the Sacrament of Confession, and from whom one receives spiritual counsel during that sacrament; praying, as appropriate, the Jesus Prayer: "Lord Jesus Christ, Son of God, have mercy on me, a sinner" (this has been—and still is—the principal devotional prayer of the Orthodox for many centuries; cf. Luke 18:13); and being alert in spiritual warfare (James 4:7), ever aware of the possibility of demonic delusion (2 Cor. 11:14; 1 Peter 5:8).

Endeavoring to be engaged in self-sacrificial service to one's fellow human beings, with deep respect, love, and compassion for each one, all "made in the image and likeness of God" (cf. Gal. 6:2; Romans 12:15).

Endeavoring to live in respectful, awe-filled harmony with nature; seeing everywhere our Creator's miraculous craftsmanship and providential care; understanding that the innate goodness of creation undergirds our entire sacramental worldview; being always thankful for, yet not being overly attached to, the good things of this world.

Witnessing to others about Christ and the glory and richness of life in his holy Church, especially through living an exemplary life of faith and virtue—through the holiness, quiet joy, and peacefulness of our Christ-filled lives; and through inviting people to church services.

Every endeavor to follow Jesus more closely is accomplished through synergistically joining our will with his will (Phil. 2:12–13), and with the grace of the Holy Spirit (1 Cor. 6:19).

Key elements of the Orthodox ethos and way of life are conveyed in the prayers normally prayed in preparation for receiving Holy Communion. For example, from the Prayer of St. Basil the Great (Archbishop of Neocaesarea, central Asia Minor; later fourth century):

Receive me, O Lord Who loves mankind, as You received the sinful woman, the thief, the publican, and the prodigal son. Take away the heavy burden of my sins, O You Who takes away the sins of the world, and heals our infirmities, and calls to Yourself all who are weary and heavy-laden and gives them rest. O You Who came not to call the righteous but sinners to repentance, cleanse me from all stain of body and soul, and teach me to fulfill holiness in reverent fear of You, so that with the witness of my conscience pure, I may receive a portion of Your Holy Gifts, and be united to Your holy Body and precious Blood, and may have You, with Your Father and Your Holy Spirit, dwelling and abiding in me.

Highlights of Responses from Other Christian Traditions

THE IMPORTANCE OF RESOURCES FOR SPIRITUAL GROWTH: David Ford, our Orthodox CP, notes the emphasis in the Orthodox Christian tradition on the church providing rich resources for spiritual growth for their parishioners, proposing that "following Jesus" includes "participating regularly in the prayer-filled and Scripture-filled liturgical/sacramental life of the church; entering with humility and awe into the majesty and beauty of the communal worship of God in church services; participating in the alternating rhythms of feasting and fasting according to the patterns designated in the church year."

Ford also proposes that Christians should endeavor "to be engaged in self-sacrificial service to one's fellow human beings, with deep respect, love, and compassion for each one, all 'made in the image of and likeness of God' (cf. Gal. 6:2; Romans 12:15)," which includes "living out the commandments of Jesus."

Much appreciation was expressed by the other CPs for the strong emphasis within the Orthodox tradition on providing Christians with resources for spiritual growth, while embracing, at least in principle, a both/and position that includes a dual focus on the importance of both drawing on resources for spiritual growth and keeping the commandments of Jesus. But a question is raised as to the balance, or lack thereof, that the Orthodox tradition has struck between these two poles.

A POSSIBLE IMBALANCE DETECTED: Concern was expressed by some CPs that, in practice, the Orthodox tradition does not adequately focus on the "keeping the commandments" pole of this both/and duality. For example, Wesley Granberg-Michaelson, our Reformed CP, perceives that in many Orthodox churches "The Bible's critique of corporate sin and the thirst for God's desired justice seems blurred."

This concern includes the observation that if one examines the curricular requirements for seminary education in the Orthodox tradition, an in-depth study of ethics appears to be optional, thereby suggesting that seminary graduates have not adequately formulated a personal ethic that includes a compendium of Christian values to which they are committed and beliefs as to which actions foster these values and which actions are destructive of these values.

This concern needs to be addressed in future conversations.

Questions for Future Conversations

Q1: Do you believe that Christians need to create a good balance between providing means for providing Christians with resources for spiritual growth and providing means for living out the commandments of Jesus? If you believe this is important, has your tradition created such a good balance? If not, what steps does your tradition need to take to correct an imbalance?

Q2: Do you agree that worshipers within your tradition need to formulate a personal ethic that includes a compendium of Christian values to which they are committed and beliefs as to which actions foster these values and which actions are destructive of these values? If you disagree, why?

What I Learned from Other Christian Traditions

Dear Conversation Partners,

Glory to Jesus Christ!

I'd like to thank each of you again for your very thoughtful, insightful, and appreciative responses to my attempt to provide at least a glimpse into the riches of Orthodox spiritual life in 1500 words! I'm very encouraged and inspired by your positive interest in Orthodoxy's understanding of following Jesus through having heartfelt intimate communion with him, as well as our cosmic sacramental worldview, which undergirds our great concern for environmental issues; our vibrant communion with the Saints, including our special love and gratitude for Mary the Theotokos; the Icons as windows into heaven; the very deep historical grounding of the Orthodox tradition; and the constant calling and aspiration to live in holiness in thought and action, with the ultimate goal of *theosis*—participating in the very life of God himself through his uncreated energies. To the extent that many of you indicated that you had been relatively unaware of these aspects of the Orthodox tradition as a whole, I am all the more motivated to try to make these treasures more widely known, so that more people may find benefit in them.

I'd also like to especially thank those of you who pointed out that my essay did not give much attention to the crucially important realm of self-sacrificial service to others—especially to those suffering from various forms of economic and/or social oppression and injustice. The particular emphasis that your traditions place on this aspect of following Jesus is certainly something that can and should inspire Orthodox Christians in general to take a more active role in combatting injustice—especially as we have the long historical experience of many centuries, going back to the Constantinian era, during which our church has worked to alleviate suffering and poverty through establishing hospitals, almshouses, homes for destitute new mothers and repentant prostitutes, and so on, as well as providing charitable assistance for poor widows. The Orthodox Church also gradually impacted the legal system of the Empire, as the state came to incorporate ecclesiastical canons into its legal code. The legal code promulgated by Emperor St. Justinian the Great (sixth century) remains the foundation of nearly all of Western law. One example of Christian influence in this code is the equalizing of penalties for adultery for both men and women. The East Roman (Byzantine) Empire also had an outstanding health care system, in which doctors treated the poor for free, while charging those who were well-off.

So even though Orthodoxy is a small minority in North America, it's certainly very important for us Orthodox Christians to keep trying to bring relief to those with material needs, as well as to influence the institutions, values, and spiritual well-being of our surrounding society.

May we all be praying to our all-compassionate Lord Jesus for his clear guidance concerning what he would have each of us do along these lines, and for his grace to empower and sustain our efforts.

Thanks again for your input. Looking forward to more conversation!

Sincerely yours, in Christ,

David Ford

II. THE ROMAN CATHOLIC TRADITION
CHRISTINA WASSELL

Following Jesus As a Traditional Roman Catholic

There is an ancient maxim, "*Lex orandi, lex credendi, lex vivendi.*" Loosely translated, this means, *The law of praying is the law of believing is the law of living.* While this captures a universal truth, it has become a motto of significance for traditionally minded Roman Catholics. Our family has been attending the Traditional Latin Mass (TLM) for almost 3 years, and it has propelled us into a radically new place of belief and practice, one we had perhaps not dared to hope for. I humbly offer here just a bit of what it means to follow Jesus as traditional Roman Catholics.

LEX ORANDI

When our family converted to Catholicism in 2010, we had worked our way through a gamut of Protestant traditions, moving steadily toward more liturgy as we went. We experienced everything from home Bible churches to mainline denominations. We finally settled at an Episcopalian church that embraced rather high Anglican sensibilities about worship. We received the Eucharist kneeling, sang from the beautiful English hymnody, and enjoyed a rich sense of the liturgical year as it moved through seasons of feasting and fasting.

When one comes from a "high church" context, it can be jarring to convert to Catholicism. It was the theology of the Eucharist and the sacraments that drew us to Rome. Reading and study and prayer confirmed for us that God was drawing us to the Roman Catholic Church. Yet our visits to many average Catholic parishes often had us shaking in our boots. The Masses felt "hokey" and at times irreverent. The music was abysmal, and while it was not impossible to find priests who could preach a good homily, these visits often smacked a little too much of campfire singalongs for our Anglican palettes. While we had made an intellectual and theological leap of faith toward the tradition that would give us the Transubstantiated Body of Christ, it felt like moving to the desert. It was belief in the sacraments that fed us, along with spiritual reading and the scaffolding of Catholic piety. We found a Cathedral parish where the Masses weren't that bad and hunkered down.

While we had no doubts about our choice to convert, and while we were growing in our Catholic faith, there was a lingering empty feeling around our actual experience of worship at Mass. The otherworldly notes that ring out in the human heart when a truly transcendent kind of worship takes place were far and few between. The "summer of shame" in 2018 brought a new toxicity to what it meant to be Catholic in the United States, with the news of the sex scandals involving then Cardinal McCarrick and his cronies across the US. Our hearts were broken. We certainly believe that the Church can be chastised by God, and that some remnant of the faithful are called to repent and do penance for a wayward bride of Christ (see the Old Testament for plenty of examples . . . Oh Israel!), but we also feared that like so many families around us, we would fail to keep our children in the Church. We were engaged in a fierce battle against the culture with our dear Catholic friends, but this battle wasn't truly led by our Catholic priests and bishops.

As laypeople we homeschooled, we prayed together, and we dug into the faith with our kids and our friends, keeping time with the year the Church lays out. We aimed to rebuild authentic Catholic culture centered on Christ and the good life he offers. And indeed we did this! The domestic church we kept in our home, along with our likeminded friends, yielded a robust Catholic life full of fireside singing, delicious homemade meals shared with friends on feast days, dancing, storytelling, games, and resurrecting Old-World Catholic traditions. But sadly, this counterculutural push to follow Jesus fizzled at Sunday Mass. We met our Lord there in the bread and wine made flesh and blood, but our offering of worship never felt quite worthy of our King and our God. What we believed theologically and lived "on the ground" with our community versus what happened at Sunday Mass did not keep stride. In our weakness, we complained. We longed for more. We grumbled and lamented about the state of things. Then, almost on a whim, we visited a new Fraternity of St. Peter (FSSP) parish dedicated to celebrating the Traditional Latin Mass. And everything changed.

Lex Credendi

In a technical sense, the Roman Catholic Church teaches that what happens on the altar at the Novus Ordo Mass (the "new order of the Mass" instituted after Vatican II around 1970 worldwide) is the same thing as what happens on the altar at the Traditional Latin Mass (which endured essentially as-is since circa AD 600, with many elements dating to the first century). All faithful Catholics assert that what happens at Mass is the unbloody re-presentation of Christ's sacrifice at Calvary. The priest is there *in persona Christi*, or as a stand-in for the one true priest, Jesus Christ, truly God and truly man. He offers the bread and the wine, each in turn, to show the separation of body from blood on the cross which resulted in Christ's death. When the priest says the words Christ spoke at the Last Supper, that bread and wine *becomes Christ* as perfect victim, offered for your sins and for mine in the mystery of the Eucharist. It happens here on earth at every Mass, at a given place and time, but when it happens we step "outside of time" and enter once again mystically into the perfect sacrifice at Calvary.

Catholics assert that true religion needs sacrifice. Sacrifice must involve gifts offered to God which are then destroyed and consumed. In the same way that so many aspects of Jewish faith are brought to a fulfillment and a completion in Christ, the Holy Sacrifice of the Mass is a new and perfect form of the sacrifice the Jewish people had been offering to God for eons. The whole point of Mass for Catholics is what happens at this moment on the altar. The music can be great. The sermon can be helpful. But this sacrifice is why we show up. This sacrifice is the praxis of our religion.

While our family understood (if imperfectly!) this theology of the Mass, attending the TLM answered our longing for a fitting form for our worship. This sigh of relief, however, was merely the beginning of a true transformation of our faith. When the *lex Orandi* changed for us in the TLM, the *lex Cre-*

dendi followed, just as the maxim describes. Without expecting it, we were drawn deeper into the wonder and mystery of the Eucharist and of following Jesus.

It would take another whole essay to describe the differences between the post Vatican II Mass and the Mass of ages, but let me skim the surface. In the TLM the priest spends the vast majority of the Mass facing the altar, with his back to the people. He is at the head of the congregation, and we are all facing God. The priest's personality essentially disappears in this Mass, allowing the *in persona Christi* aspect of his role to emerge. The new Mass, with the priest behind the altar table facing the people, invites a kind of showmanship, with the priest highly aware of his "command of the crowd," using voice and eye contact as features of the Mass, and creating a closed loop focused more on the horizontal experience of faith in a community than on the vertical experience of worshiping God on high.

The TLM is brimming with silence. While the new Mass follows a "call and response" format where the priest says essentially everything out loud and the congregation joins in or responds, there are many places in the TLM where the priest is praying quietly, only to God. The congregation can follow along in missals, but the silence invites a meditative prayer hard to find at the new Mass, where we learn to unite our own sacrifices to Christ's on the altar. The TLM uses primarily Gregorian chant. This other-worldly music was created for worship and draws the heart and mind up to God in a way that impoverished Catholic worship tunes just . . . cannot. The TLM offers confession throughout the Mass, and the faithful avail themselves of this sacrament frequently. As we approach Communion, we want to be forgiven and prepared to receive our Lord. Desperately aware of our need for grace, we pray at each Mass (as the Centurion did), "Lord, I am not worthy that you should enter under my roof, but only say the word and my soul shall be healed." We only receive our Lord kneeling in humility, and on the tongue. Only the consecrated hands of the priest feed him to us, taking such reverent care not to drop a single crumb, as each crumb is the whole of the body, blood, soul, and divinity of the Lord.

Lᴇx Vɪᴠᴇɴᴅɪ

Before we found the Traditional Latin Mass, our experience of following Jesus was, in a sense, upside down. Now, our experience of Christ *flows out from the Mass*. The Mass itself, in its structure, its music, its gestures, its engagement of all the human senses, continually teaches us about Jesus Christ and his Church. We meet him there. The Eucharist, the centerpiece of the Mass and the source and summit of our faith, shines more brilliantly for us than it ever did, illuminating our efforts to follow Jesus.

Highlights from Other Christian Traditions

Aɴ Iᴍᴘᴏʀᴛᴀɴᴛ, Oꜰᴛᴇɴ Nᴇɢʟᴇᴄᴛᴇᴅ Dɪᴍᴇɴꜱɪᴏɴ ᴏꜰ Fᴏʟʟᴏᴡɪɴɢ Jᴇꜱᴜꜱ: Our Catholic CP, Christina Wassell, describes herself as "only a housewife," rather than "a scholar, theologian, teacher, or leader in my tradition" (as are the other CPs). But who Christina is enables her to focus on a dimension of following Jesus that is too-often neglected in all Christian traditions: establishing and nurturing a "Domestic Church." Christina describes her Domestic Church as follows:

> As laypeople we homeschooled, we prayed together, and we dug into the faith with our kids and our friends, keeping time with the year the Church lays

out. We aimed to rebuild authentic Catholic culture centered on Christ and the good life He offers. And indeed we did this! The domestic church we kept in our home, along with our likeminded friends, yielded a robust Catholic life full of fireside singing, delicious homemade meals shared with friends on feast days, dancing, storytelling, games, and resurrecting Old-World Catholic traditions.

The context for Christina's family living out their Domestic Church is their commitment to attending the Traditional Latin Mass (TLM) that downplays the role of the presiding priest: "the priest's . . . personality essentially disappears in the mass, allowing the *in persona Christi* aspect of his role to emerge."

A number of the other CPs express appreciation for aspects of "TLM spirituality," although a concern is expressed that it makes a false choice between the "vertical experience of worshiping God on high" and the "horizontal experience of faith in a community" (it is both/and; not either/or). But an even deeper concern is expressed, which elaborates on Christina's characterization of "the Roman Catholic Church as a church in crisis."

A DEEP DIVISION WITHIN ROMAN CATHOLICISM: As suggested by David Gushee, our Baptist CP, the present division within the Roman Catholic Church can be traced to "the innovations unleashed by and through the Vatican II conference (1962–1965), with many millions of Catholics cherishing aspects of Vatican II and others resistant to any and all of its changes."

A belief expressed by a number of our CPs is that, while those within the TLM movement may indeed embrace the teaching of the *Catechism of the Catholic Church* that calls Catholics to "social service," they have too often succumbed to a narrow view of "social service" that leaves little room for addressing "systemic social problems" that are at the root of many current injustices in America, resulting in the "political theology" of the TLM movement being "reactionary politics" that "buys into an entire conservative [political] agenda" (to quote Randall Balmer, our Anglican CP); even suggesting that "Pope Francis is a raving liberal."

The response to this criticism from those within the TLM movement is that, too often, attempts to address such systemic social problems have led Catholic Christians to compromise their Christian principles (e.g., accepting government subsidies with "strings attached" that water down the services that can be provided by Catholic hospitals and other Catholic social service entities).

A possible response to this response is that the messy political process for deciding on appropriate governmental actions is such that the results of Christians doing politics will inevitably fall short of the ideals of any Christian tradition. Therefore, Christians in any tradition should be careful not to make an "unrealizable perfect" the enemy of a "realizable good."

All of the above leads to a number of questions for future conversation, which will be posed in the next section.

Questions for Future Conversation

Q1: To what extent do you believe worshipers within the Roman Catholic tradition exemplify commitment to establishing and nurturing a "Domestic Church?" What are the strengths and limitations of such a focus? What is your perception as to the extent to which such a focus is prevalent in other Christian traditions?

Q2: What do you believe is the extent of the deep division within Roman Catholicism between the TLM movement and post-Vatican II Catholicism that is portrayed in this conversation? If you perceive such deep division, what steps should be taken to lessen this division?

Q3: What is your perception as to the extent to which Roman Catholicism, and every other Christian tradition, is not monolithic, but includes a diversity of perspectives as to what it means to follow Jesus?

Q4: Do you agree with the assessment that beliefs about "social service" within the TLM movement do not adequately address "systemic social problems," leading to a "reactionary politics" that "buys into an entire conservative political agenda?" If you disagree, explain your disagreement.

Q5: Do you agree with the claim that when Roman Catholics, or adherents to any other Christian tradition, engage in political deliberations regarding the proper role of government in serving the needs of the marginalized in society, they will have to "settle for" public policies that will not fully measure up to Christian ideals? If you do not agree with this claim, what role, if any, should Roman Catholics or other Christians play in the political realm?

What I Learned from Other Christian Traditions

Greetings in the name of Christ the King!

Once this project was underway and I was able to read the bios of all my Conversation Partners, I joked with Harold

Heie that it seemed a bit of a conspiracy to make the Catholic Church look bad, with only a housewife as her representative! I am not a scholar, theologian, teacher, or leader in my tradition the way all of you are, and so I thank you for the patience and care you took to read and respond to my post. While I have done what I can to represent my own experience and move toward first the Roman Catholic Church, and then to a more traditional community within the vast sea of Roman Catholics, I'm sure my efforts have fallen short when it comes to speaking for the Roman Catholic tradition broadly.

It was a pleasure to read all your thoughtful responses. Thank you for your honesty and your willingness to connect your own experiences of following Jesus with mine where possible, but also to address areas of disagreement frankly. The questions and critiques you raise are honest and fair. Most reveal to me that 1500 words (even with an additional 1000 added on!) are really not enough to explain both my journey *and* the broad scope of Catholicism when it comes to following the Lord. It would take another tome to address the theological differences that came up around things like the Eucharist and transubstantiation, the role of Mary the Mother of God and the saints, the all-male priesthood in the Catholic Church, Rome's take on the priesthood of all believers, and certainly the implementation of social justice through the Catholic Church in a fallen world (to name only a few). There were also more political issues raised, both in the realm of church politics and state politics, which would perhaps turn the conversation down a different path if I were really to explain myself.

Instead, let me mention a hope I have for my efforts at this daunting task. First, I hope it has come through that I would characterize the Roman Catholic Church as a church in crisis. Please know that there is a kind of humility built into the nature of being Catholic in 2021 because of the very real shortcomings of the Church evident to the whole world, since they make the headlines of major newspapers on a regular basis. This bride of Christ is sullied, tattered, and torn, bruised, and beaten from within and without. And yet, one of the weird things about being a faithful Catholic is that we are bound to stay Catholic. When we converted, I had no real idea that part of the call on our family would be to fast and pray for Holy Mother Church, and to wear a thorny crown of humiliation, which we must offer up as one more sacrifice that helps us to become like our Lord. He did warn us, to be fair, that it would be this way.

Reading all your postings was certainly fruitful for me. I learned about traditions I've scarcely heard of! I learned (perhaps again) about that push and pull we feel when we explore other traditions and allow them to be held up as a mirror opposite our own. I learned more about some of the documents that the Roman Catholic Church has been working on with many of your churches, which I've only heard mention of through the years. Perhaps most important, I've tried to really hear and mull over the shortcomings some of you identify in my tradition. I hope that the responses to your postings I can offer over the next several months will help to further flesh out our differences—and our common ground.

I want to leave you with the words (in translation) of a very old song that Christian pilgrims would sing together as they marched along the way. Our kids love to belt it out in Latin with their friends under the stars, as it would have been done long ago. It is from a very old medieval manuscript collection, *The Llibre Vermell de Montserrat*, prepared around AD 1399. I share it because I sincerely believe we are all fellow pilgrims on this road to Christ and toward the Parousia we so look forward to. I hope it captures some of the wonder that the vast array of humanity is invited to in Christ, and through his Blessed Mother.

In the love of our Lord,

Christina Wassell

Stella Splendens
(The melody is haunting, and worthy of a listen on YouTube)

Chorus:
Splendid star on the serrated mountain,
with miracles shining like a sunbeam, hear the people.

From all around they rally, rejoicing,
rich and poor, young and old,
they assemble here to see with their own eyes,
and return from it filled with grace.

Rulers and magnates of royal stripes,
the mighty of the world, having obtained indulgence
for their sin, they cry out and beating their breast
they kneel and cry thus: Ave Maria.

Prelates and barons, famous counts,
all kinds of monks and priests,
soldiers, merchants, citizens, sailors,
burghers and fishermen are recompensed here.

Peasants, ploughmen and also scribes,
advocates, stone-masons and all carpenters,
tailors and shoemakers, and weavers as well,
all kinds of craftsmen rejoice here.

THE ROMAN CATHOLIC TRADITION

Queens, countesses, illustrious ladies powerful
and maidens, teenagers and girls,
virgins, old women and widows equally,
climb this mountain; so do nuns.

All these groups assemble here to present themselves,
to remember their vows and keep them as well
by enriching this temple so that all may see this
adorning it with jewels, and return home released.

Therefore, everybody, male and female,
beseeching and cleansing our minds,
let us devoutly pray that we may really experience the glory of the Virgin,
the clemency of the Mother, and her gracefulness in heaven.

Translation by Dick Wursten

III. THE LUTHERAN TRADITION
MARK ELLINGSEN

Lutheranism: An Evangelical Catholic Way to Follow Jesus

In order to articulate Lutheranism's approach to following Jesus, we need to sort out the Lutheran self-image (at least its historical image) and appreciate the diversity within the Lutheran family. Of course it is well known that Lutherans did not originally name themselves Lutheran. That title is a function of their critics naming them, rather like Christians and Methodists got their name from their critics. The original name for the followers of Luther was Evangelical, even Evangelical [Gospel] Catholics. Thus built into the very fiber of Lutheranism is a commitment to embrace what is truly catholic in the Christian heritage, but in such a way as to highlight the gospel of grace.

As a result of these commitments, Lutheranism has been characterized by several distinct strands. Its catholic orientation permits and even mandates the presence of this diversity. Although any characterization in terms of typology can distort, I think that most students of Lutheranism would agree that we can distinguish between its Pietistic strands and its more Confessional strands (referring to adherence to the teachings of the Lutheran Confessions, *The Book of Concord*).

Although virtually all Lutherans pledge fidelity to the teaching of the Lutheran Confessions (esp. the sixteenth-century document The Augsburg Confession), the Pietist strand tends to focus so much more on the spiritual life with a program for following Jesus. This strand is also less focused on the role of the Sacraments and liturgy in Christian nurture and is more inclined to identify Lutheranism with Protestantism. A latter-day development of this strand, which we might call Liberal Protestantism, is in line with these overall commitments, though with more stress on apologetics and making following Jesus relevant to our context, with a little less focus on spirituality. My sense is that although there are regional differences, the Liberal Protestant view (combined with a conservative view of Biblical authority) is probably the dominant viewpoint in the American Lutheran pew today. I would be bold to make the claim that the Lutheran majority in American pews is comprised of a coalition of this group with the relatively smaller group of remaining Lutheran Pietists.

The Confessional side of Lutheranism is likewise diverse. First we think of Lutheran Orthodoxy, a strand which demands total fidelity to the Lutheran Confessions. This approach has more of an appreciation of the Sacramental heritage than does Pietism, and it may emphasize salvation by grace more than Pietism does, but adherents tend to think of themselves as Protestant and embrace ways of following Jesus akin to most Protestants. Proponents of this model probably dominate in The Lutheran Church—Missouri Synod and in the Wisconsin Synod.

The other Confessional model of Lutheranism might be termed Neo-Confessional or Evangelical Catholicism. This group of Lutherans reads both the Lutheran Confessions and the Bible critically, but still in a manner compatible with more liberal, open elements of the Evangelical movement. Proponents of this model share the Lutheran Orthodox model's commitment to the centrality of justification by grace, but they place more focus on Sacramental and liturgical dimensions of Christian nurture. Indeed, this commitment is so strong, along with the associated Christology and ecclesiology (or polity), that proponents of this model of Lutheranism often tend to reject identification with Protestantism. Rather, the Eastern Orthodox, Roman Catholic, and Anglo-Catholic heritages are regarded as the closest allies of this Lutheranism.

The stress on grace also leads Lutherans who operate with this model to emphasize freedom from God's law and a situational ethic, claiming to be the true heirs of Luther. This is my own impression, but since I identify with this strand, the preceding judgment about which strand is the true heir of Luther is certainly worthy of challenge. I can note that this is certainly not the dominant version of Lutheranism in the American Lutheran pew, and yet its unique perspectives on following Jesus warrant the attention of the Church catholic.

The interesting thing about these different strands and their different views of following Jesus is that historically they have usually lived together under the rubric *Lutheran*. To be sure, in some cases these disagreements have led to denominational divisions, but only in extreme cases is the Lutheranism of those from whom a group separates questioned. This is one of the senses in which we may say that Lutheranism at its best is a catholic tradition.

Liturgical-Sacramental Spirituality

Let's begin with what most Lutherans can agree concerning following Jesus: First and foremost is the conviction that the Christian life must be rooted in God's grace, that we are justified by grace alone (Romans 3:21-28; Galatians 3:10-14; *Luther's Works*, Vol. 26, p. 106; Apology of the Augsburg Confessions, IV.2-3). Following Jesus is a gift of God, for even faith is a work of the Holy Spirit (Small Catechism, II.6).

It is at this point that we can best understand the Lutheran preoccupation with the role of liturgy, Sacramentology, and the communion of saints in nurturing Christian life. Of course liturgy cannot have a sacrificial connotation (Apology of the Augsburg Confessions, XXIV.79). But this style of worship, the ancient character of the Communion of Saints and a Real Presence understanding of the sacraments (Christ coming to us and changing us [Small Catechism]) are essentially related for Lutherans to the prioritizing of salvation and living the Christian life by grace alone! They are means through which God makes us people who *want* to follow Jesus. In worship, the benefits of God are received (Apology of the Augsburg Confession, IV.49), in baptism we are born again and begin to live out our baptism (Romans 6; Large Catechism IV. 27), and in the Lord's Supper forgiveness is not only received, but in our bodies we actually receive Christ, who transforms the recipients into people who are linked to all the faithful, their strengths and their needs (Large Catechism, V.22, 70; *Luther's Works*, Vol. 35, pp. 50-52, 58, 59).

There is an openness in Lutheran teaching to accepting all seven sacraments (Apology of the Augsburg Confessions, XIII.2). And each of these rites is understood as changing the believer or at least putting him/her in a new context, which nurtures new ways of behaving.

With regard to the Church's role in nurturing Christian spirituality, Luther calls it our Mother, who begets and bears every Christian (*Luther's Works*, Vol. 51, p. 166). Again, note how Christian life has a passive element, is a life acted on by grace, born and nurtured by God through the Church. Of course, we are not alone in following Jesus. In addition to acknowledging support from the Church and Sacraments, Luther was open to invoking angels and Mary (whom he called the Mother of God) (*Luther's Works*, Vol. 42, p. 113; *Ibid.*, Vol. 21, pp. 328-29). All the saints may pray for us, he claimed (*Smalcald Articles*, II.25f.).

The sacraments, the liturgy, and the communion of saints all aid Christians in following Jesus. Along with preaching and Bible study they contribute to making such a lifestyle not something to aspire to, but making it a gift, transforming us into people who joyfully, spontaneously live as the kind of people God wants the faithful to be.

Following Jesus in Accord with Ecumenical Consensus

As I've noted in my previous two responses, a lot of the ways of following Jesus posited by the Pietist and Liberal Protestant strands of Lutheranism correspond to Orthodox and Catholic visions of following Jesus. And these strands also share commonalities, along with Lutheran Orthodoxy, with most Protestant denominations. Certainly, the Catholic or Orthodox heritage is reflected in the qualified openness to Synergism one finds affirmed in official Lutheran documents. With warnings, the synergistic joining of our will with God's grace is not rejected (*Formula of Concord*, SD II.90). Of course, this openness is endorsed along with the strong Lutheran commitment to prevenient grace (the belief that grace precedes any synergistic cooperation), for the Holy Spirit is given credit for our faith and for the surrender of the will to God (Romans 3:21-28; Galatians 3:10-14; *Luther's Works*, Vol. 26, p. 106; *Small Catechism*, II.6). In this context, even embracing *theosis* would raise no problems from the Evangelical Catholic wing of Lutheranism, as Luther himself seems sometimes to have endorsed the concept (*Complete Sermons*, Vol. 4/2, pp. 279-80). And the theme of being united with Christ, a theme also typical of Mysticism, is prominent of much Lutheran literature, though not widely known in the pews (*Smalcald Articles*, III.13; Apology of The Augsburg Confession, IV.72).

In accord with the Catholic and Orthodox heritage, along with most Protestant denominational traditions, there are times when Lutherans express openness to measuring how well we follow Jesus by the keeping of the Commandments (*Formula of Concord* SD VII; *Large Catechism*, I.Con), even measuring growth in the Christian life this way (*Formula of Concord*, SD IV.31-33). In fact, the idea of striving for perfection (implied in striving to live in purity and in accord with the process of *theosis*) is embraced in segments of Lutheran Pietism (Philip Spener, *Pia Desideria*, 2).

Although Luther himself was critical of Pentecostal experience (*Luther's Works*, Vol. 40, pp. 83, 90), and some Lutheran denominations discourage the practice (esp. The Wisconsin Evangelical Lutheran Church), increasingly many American Lutherans have come to embrace the validity of speaking in tongues—as long as insights gained through the experience do not outweigh Biblical authority and the experience of the gift of tongues is not privileged over other spiritual gifts (1 Corinthians 13-14; Paul Opsahl, ed., *The Holy Spirit in the Life of the Church*). But not only do Lutherans have a strong doctrine of the Holy Spirit, giving the Spirit credit for working all things pertinent to salvation and following Jesus (Small Catechism, II.6), as we'll note below, they also seem open to experiencing something like the ecstasy (losing oneself in the Spirit) that Pentecostals claim when, in following Jesus, the faithful simply do so spontaneously without prodding or calculation.

Lutherans also join with most Protestants in embracing the idea that all who are baptized, all who follow Jesus, are priests. Christians who follow Jesus are priests, for they have been dedicated to living lives in which they perform the sacrifice of dying to their sin and rising to serve Christ and the neighbor (*Luther's Works*, Vol. 31, p. 53; *Ibid.*, Vol. 36, p. 145; Apology of the Augsburg Confession, XXIV.26). Lutherans do this in living their baptisms as people now born again in the baptismal waters (note the Sacramental orientation at this point) (*Luther's Works*, Vol. 35, p. 31). Another affirmation that Lutherans share with many Protestants (especially Baptists and Holiness Christians) is to regard following Jesus in terms of the need to repent (*Weimar Ausgabe*, Vol. 12, p. 591; the first thesis of The Ninety-Five Theses calls for daily repentance).

An additional aspect of the Lutheran version of following Jesus that converges with many traditions pertains to social ethics. Although it is not just followers of Jesus who are expected to do this (as per the Lutheran Two-Kingdom Ethic, see *Complete Sermons of Martin Luther*, Vol. 3/2, p. 319), Lutherans think Christians are people who will always have a concern about justice for the poor (*Luther's Works*, Vol. 9, p. 19; Large Catechism, I.7; Amos 8:4ff). There are a lot of areas in which most participants in this conversation can find agreement with the Lutheran heritage. But the Lutheran emphasis on freedom in the Christian life may be problematic for many, at least if conversation partners do not try to cut through stereotypes and really try to empathize with what is at stake in these distinctively Lutheran commitments.

Christian Freedom: Are Lutherans Unique in These Ways of Following Jesus? Can Other Christian Heritages Entertain These Proposals?

Freedom from the demands of the Law was the crucial agenda associated with Luther's stress on justification by grace through faith (the most important of all Christian teachings according to Lutheran theology [Apology of the Augsburg Confession, IV.2-3]). Another commitment that makes being set free from the Law's demands absolutely essential is Luther's contention that we sin in everything we do (Romans 7; *Luther's Works*, Vol. 25, p. 375; *Ibid.*, Vol. 33, pp. 67, 115,

176.). For since he understands sin as concupiscence/selfishness, it follows that it is impossible to stop sinning on this side of the Fall (*Ibid.*, Vol. 31, 9, 10, 13). Scientific research on the human brain seems to bear out this Augustinian insight. It seems that one of the reasons we do good or love is because our brains are rewarded for such activities with the flow of the good-feeling brain chemical dopamine (David Brinn, "Israeli researchers discover gene for altruism"). In short, even the best human behavior is selfish.

With this awareness that everything we do is a sin, it follows that the best Christians can be is *simul iustus et peccator* (100% saint and 100% sinner) (Romans 7:14-18; *Luther's Works*, Vol. 32, p. 111; *Ibid.*, Vol. 27, p. 230). This is a freeing insight, as it entails the awareness that we are loved by God, even despite all our sin and selfishness. Lutherans know that all humanity is affirmed, that we can all "come as we are" to God. This insight also led Luther to refer to an awareness that the best the Christian can do is "sin bravely" (1 Timothy 1:13; *Luther's Works.*, Vol. 48, pp. 281-82)!

At this point, we need to clarify precisely what the first Reformer meant by this phrase. This is not the "cheap grace" Bonhoeffer (*The Cost of Discipleship*) worried about while in dialogue with a Lutheran Orthodox theology in his day, prone to separate Justification and Sanctification almost like the Holiness Movement does. Rather, for Luther you only sin bravely when you do not give in to concupiscence, when you boldly live a sacrificial, sin-denying life (live your baptism) but do so with the awareness that even then you are still sinning, that all good done is a function of God working in and through you (*Complete Sermons*, Vol. 4, p. 367). This sort of humility about what you can do on your own requires that God must be given all the credit when it comes to our following Jesus.

These commitments lead the first Reformer and his tradition to avoid exhorting the faithful how to live with guidelines, commands, or discipline (though as we have noted, especially the Pietist and Lutheran Orthodox segments of the heritage allow for it). The concern is that if you direct someone how to live, you lay more guilt on them, and since we are sinning in all we do, you set them up for failure. Christians are free from the Law (Galatians 3:13; 5:1; Romans 7:4ff; *Luther's Works*, Vol. 31, pp. 333-77). There is no need for it for those who already know their sin, for good works are spontaneous (Ephesians 2:10; *Luther's Works*, Vol. 31, pp. 367-68; *Complete Sermons*, Vol. 1/2, p. 316). Freedom from the Law also entails the possibility of a Situational Ethic (Genesis 22; *Luther's Works*, Vol. 5, p. 150; *Complete Sermons*, Vol. 3/1, p. 61).

Followers of Jesus are often said to be caught up in the loving arms of our Lord. Although it is true that like most Protestants, Lutherans often refer to justification and salvation merely as the proclamation of forgiveness (*Formula of Concord*, Ep III.7; *Ibid.* SD III.9), Luther and his tradition also refer to justification as being united with Christ (*Smalcald Articles*, II.13; Apology of The Augsburg Confession, IV.72). To be in Christ is like being married to him (Galatians 2:20; Ephesians 3:17; Song of Solomon; *Luther's Works*, Vol. 31, pp. 351ff). In a good marriage, the qualities of your mate begin to rub off on you. Thus, to be married to Christ is to share his goodness and love.

When you live in a family with a lover whose love works on you, the loved one does not have to tell you what to do to please him/her. You just sort of know. True human love is spontaneous. Imagine then what God's love can do to you. In fact, when you are in love (fall in love, note the passivity) it is like an ecstatic experience. You lose yourself. Should we not expect it to be that way in the arms of Jesus? This is another reason why Lutherans claim that there is no need to teach Christians how to follow Jesus. It will just happen spontaneously when you are living with Jesus. And likewise, a Situational Ethic makes sense in a family context. You love each of your kids and your spouse differently from the way you love others, and no one else loves their families in precisely the same way as you love yours. Indeed, sometimes telling a lie to boost a lover's confidence is the right and loving thing to do. Are there not times when the right thing to do is to break the Commandments (such as Bonhoeffer's efforts to kill a human being [Hitler])?

Research on the brain seems to bear out Lutheran insights about the spontaneity of good works. It seems that when the brain is engaged in spiritual exercises, the front part of the brain is activated (the prefrontal cortex). And the brain facilitates the exercise of this cortex and the new neural connections that emerge as a result of its activity by secreting the good-feeling brain chemicals dopamine and oxytocin. It also seems that these brain chemicals are especially conducive to stimulating social behavior (Andrew Newberg and Mark Waldman, *How God Changes Your Brain*, pp. 55–56; Patty Van Cappellen, et al, "Effects of oxytocin administration on spirituality and emotional responses to medication"; Marcello Ceboroio, "Trust, Generosity, Affection: The Benefits of Oxytocin"). In short, neurobiology teaches us that faith inclines human beings to do good works spontaneously!

The good feelings of joy and contentment that these faith-related brain chemicals afford fit nicely with the Lutheran emphasis on joy in the Christian life (*Luther's Works*, Vol. 44, pp. 26, 29; Ibid., Vol. 17, p. 258). This joy permeates all the activities Lutherans identify with following Jesus: Bible study, prayer, and evangelism. They are not serious, weighty duties, but just plain fun! And the dopamine that comes with faith also affords energy, the kind of energy required by the Lutheran expectation that action in the moment is urgent, for Lutheranism reminds the faithful that every moment can be a moment in which the kingdom of God is realized (Small Catechism).

We have noted that Lutherans can at least provisionally embrace most everything other churches say about following Jesus. Can the rest of the catholic tradition also embrace the freedom, spontaneity, and fun that Lutherans often associate with following Jesus?

Highlights of Responses from Other Christian Traditions

THE JOYS OF FREEDOM AND SPONTANEITY: Mark Ellingsen, our Lutheran CP, acknowledges the diversity within the Lutheran tradition between its "pietistic strand" that "focuses more on the spiritual life and a program for following Jesus" and its more "confessional strand" that includes greater emphasis on "the role of the Sacraments and liturgy in Christian nurture" (noting that he situates himself within the confessional strand).

But, granting this diversity, Ellingsen strongly asserts that "most Lutherans can agree" that "first and foremost in their understanding of what it means to follow Jesus" is "the conviction that the Christian life must be rooted in God's grace" and that this conviction entails an emphasis on "freedom from God's law and a situational ethic" that finds expression in "freedom and spontaneity" that brings much "joy" (even "plain fun"). But this raises the question as to whether there are boundaries to the exercise of freedom and spontaneity.

POSSIBLE LIMITS ON FREEDOM AND SPONTANEITY: A number of the other CPs express appreciation for Ellingsen's emphasis on freedom and spontaneity in following Jesus. For example, Wesley Granberg-Michaelson, our Reformed CP, suggests that Ellingsen's call for freedom from the law and his embrace of spontaneity are antidotes to the tendency of some within the Reformed tradition to make rules to follow that are "onerous, excessive, and guilt-producing."

But significant concern is expressed by a number of CPs that this focus on freedom and responsibility can lead to behaviors that are destructive of God's redemptive purposes. Therefore, in the words of David Gushee, our Baptist CP, serious consideration must be given to the "concrete moral teachings of Jesus" that have a "law or rule-like dimension."

Drawing on my own experience in the 1950s relative to the impact of a proposal for a situational ethic from Joseph Fletcher in his very influential book *Situation Ethics*, I express concern that a focus on "freedom and spontaneity" too easily leads to "irresponsible" behavior. For example, prompted by Fletcher's proposal to just "do the loving thing," some women in communal settings were being sexually abused in the name of love. A claim to be doing the loving thing in a given situation is not self-authenticating.

Questions for Future Conversation

Q1: If you believe there are "boundaries" to the expression on "freedom and spontaneity" in Christian living, what are those "boundaries?"

Q2: Is it possible that there is legitimacy in BOTH a focus on "freedom and spontaneity" AND the need for law-like boundaries on that freedom and spontaneity that reflect the life and teachings of Jesus? If so, how does one create an appropriate balance between these two poles?

Q3: Ellingsen suggests that our differing ways of following Jesus may reflect differences in "who we are": "Some of us are or want to become more serious, more organized, more methodical, more activist, and gravitate to those biblical themes which provide concrete guidance, while others (like Lutherans) love the biblical themes stressing freedom and spontaneity because such themes are a little more comforting to those who are guilt-ridden or who want to be more care-free, fun-loving, and go with the flow." Do you agree with Ellingsen? If not, why not? If you agree, what are the implications for striking the "balance" sought for in Q2?

Is Spontaneity and Freedom from the Law a Legitimate Option in the Church Catholic?

I really appreciated the dialogue with all my partners (the new friends I'm making), and my responses to each will indicate in more depth my appreciation and thoughts about your insightful reflections. I am struck by how two elements of the Lutheran heritage seem to be met with appreciation— either the Sacramental heritage or the Lutheran Confessional stress on freedom, spontaneity, along with joy. Of course, none of my conversational partners can fully sign on to the freedom from the law theme, and the reservations raised are not surprises. Their hesitation about such themes is nothing new to a Lutheran like me who travels in ecumenical circles. But in the traditions of Lutheran (maybe Norwegian) stubbornness, I want to raise the question of my original contribution in a more pointed way, as I am still not sure I got a direct answer from all of the CPs: If I were invited to preach in your churches (assuming it was an official and legitimate invitation), could I preach on freedom from the Law (in the Lutheran Confessional sense) and on the spontaneity of good works, even suggesting to the congregation that they might sin bravely for our Lord and sometimes need to break the Law for the sake of love? To be sure, those themes are not characteristic of any denomination except mine. But are these characteristically Lutheran themes still deemed legitimately Christian enough to be espoused and validly taught in your communities? Lutheranism's catholicity, I've tried to point out to date, is able to embrace all the themes precious to my partners (in some cases through its Pietistic and in other cases through its Confessional strands, allowing for this sort of reconciled diversity). Lutheranism is big enough for most things your tradition might teach (I'll point out to you in the months ahead how Lutherans can even get along with those who don't teach the Sacraments like us). How big (how catholic) is your tradition's tent?

If we are all big tents, how do we reconcile the diversity and make sense of it? I was moved by the responses of most everyone, suggesting that the reason your tradition could not unequivocally embrace Lutheran spontaneity and freedom was related either to differences in personal traits of our founders or to a sense that more realism or skepticism about the complexities of life, its seriousness, needs to be taken into account. These are exciting insights for me. If we conceded that all our various ways of following Jesus have some biblical authorization, could it be that our denominational differences in following Jesus relate to the fact that some of us are or want to become more serious, more organized, more methodical, more activist, and gravitate to those biblical themes that provide concrete guidance, while others (like Lutherans) love the biblical themes stressing freedom and spontaneity because such themes are a little more comforting to those who are guilt-ridden or who want to be more carefree and fun-loving, and go with the flow? Extended families and communities (maybe even the Church) need both types of people and should be sensitive in ministering to both groups.

We so beautifully balance out each other. For all their pessimism about human nature (its sinfulness), Lutherans have this naïve confidence that God's grace changes lives without any help. And while the rest of the Christian world (Reformed and some Baptist friends possibly excluded) cannot fully buy the Augustinian pessimism about human nature as Lutherans do, the majority of us Christians are more realistic about what grace can accomplish on its own without the aid of the Law. Our pessimism/realism and optimism/naïveté balance out each other in different ways. Realists and optimists need each other in order to thrive.

Have you heard of the old adage of how you can tell the difference between a Lutheran pastor and other clergy in town? Most clergy (in the days before the 60s) had to purchase their alcohol anonymously or with great care, while the Lutheran pastor could buy all the alcohol he/she wanted and even tell people in town about it. Could our denominational differences be as simple as different ways of appropriating biblical themes for different personality types (or at least for different people with different visions of what kind of people the world needs followers of Jesus to be)? I am reminded here of Luther's comments about the two kinds of Word of God—what applies to me and my situation and what does not (Luther's Works, Vol. 35, p. 170). The key to our dialogue might be as simple as understanding our dialogue partner to be applying a biblical theme (a Word of God) that does not apply to some of the rest of us, but recognizing that that theme is still legitimate Word of God. Can you buy that, colleagues, when it comes to freedom from the Law, sinning bravely, and a situational ethic?

How can this appreciation of biblical diversity all fit together? Maybe we can solve it together. I'm taken by the potential that quantum physics offers. In order to explain the paradox of how an electron can be both wave and particle (a logical contradiction) Werner Heisenberg developed the concept of complementarity, which he thought applicable to religious matters as well (*Physics and Philosophy*, pp. 135, P.S. 23). Like waves and particles, could there be such complementarity between the favorite Lutheran themes and those most precious to your tradition? We might have fun exploring those questions together. Already I've got a couple of partners who tell me they are ready to explore having fun with me and my Lutheran heritage. To them I suggest that we start making plans regarding how to try to concretize these prospects at the denominational level. And all of your collective comments indicate areas in which there is convergence between each of our heritages. Maybe with more of the individual dialogue I hope to have with each of you, we can have fun identifying other possible topics for more conversations, other candidates for complementarity.

IV. THE ANABAPTIST TRADITION
MICHAEL KING

Amid Complexities, Five Things Many Anabaptist-Mennonites Emphasize

Yes, I *will* summarize five Anabaptist-Mennonite emphases. But I don't dare try before addressing complexities of doing so when so many groups stress so many different things.

We can link *some* Anabaptist-Mennonitisms back to Swiss Anabaptism. Even as approaches to Anabaptist origins and contemporary implications vary (as historians contest whether "polygenesis," "monogenesis," or some blend best explains Anabaptist beginnings), noteworthy was the 1525 Zurich move by leaders such as Conrad Grebel and George Blaurock to rebaptize each other. They and others called for rebaptizing adults committed to a "believers church" and by 1527 produced the Schleitheim Confession summarizing early Swiss Anabaptist beliefs. They also contributed to a believers church shadow: If only believers belong in the church and are to rightly live Jesus' teachings, there is potential for endless schism over who is the true believer.

* * *

Today, among many Anabaptist-Mennonite groups, some include the name *Anabaptist*, some *Mennonite*, some neither. Yet they are broadly part of Mennonitism, whether in North America or worldwide. Mennonites gained their name as disciples of the 1500s former Roman Catholic priest, the Frisian (Netherlands) Menno Simons. Other Anabaptist groups, such as Church of the Brethren, Brethren in Christ, and Hutterites may have varying links to Mennonites but involve different branchings-out of Anabaptism.

Then there are the Amish. Though they diverged in the 1600s, their roots are Swiss Anabaptist. The Amish are part of my family lineage some generations back. Despite their split from branches of Anabaptism with which I'm most connected, their plain and simple living commitments make their own contributions. The Amish have sometimes intertwined with Mennonite streams as wings of Mennonites and Amish have migrated back and forth. Thus, for example, someone like my aunt Evelyn King Mumaw could tell of how, after her family was put out of its Mennonite wing, they attended Conestoga Amish Mennonite Church.

* * *

The point is not the details but that one could go on and on about who believed what, belonged to whom when and for how long, evicted one group or joined another. As addressed in my response to Orthodoxy, long unfolding Anabaptist-Mennonite diversification seems only to have gathered momentum in Mennonite Church USA, to which I belong. This has led to MC USA losing nearly half of its members since its formation in 2002. Despite the goal—heal divisions and merge two prior denominations—MC USA faces continuing challenges, and the merger split off MC Canada from what had been a binational church.

As touched on in my response to Ford on Orthodoxy, a significant, though not only, factor heightening tensions has involved LGBTQ+IA-related decisions. I once pastored a congregation the denomination later excommunicated when it was perceived to have moved too far toward inclusion; I was saddened when delegates of another congregation I was then pastoring voted for eviction. In 2015 I was an MC USA seminary dean when the university to which it belonged navigated both internal divisions and the wider denominational tumult in moving toward a more inclusive hiring policy. In 2015 and beyond, many congregations and some conferences—regional and/or affiliative clusters of congregations into which MC USA is subdivided—shifted loyalties to different entities or left MC USA entirely.

* * *

So what *do* Mennonites believe amid ongoing wrestlings? Key is the *1995 Mennonite Confession of Faith in Mennonite Perspective* and its summary of 24 principles MC USA formally affirms. But what of Anabaptist-Mennonite streams that have left MC USA or in some cases never joined?

For example, CMC, formerly Conservative Mennonite Conference, now labeling itself an "evangelical Anabaptist denomination with headquarters in Irwin, Ohio," offers alternative statements of faith on theology and practice.

LMC—"A fellowship of Anabaptist churches," formerly Lancaster Mennonite Conference—was until recently the largest of MC USA's conferences. Now LMC states commitment to the 1995 COF but doesn't mention in summarizing Anabaptist-Mennonite history its departure from the denomination of which it was once such a large part.

Acronyms such as CMC or LMC in place of *Mennonite* matter. They signal preference to emphasize evangelical and/or Anabaptist over Mennonite components.

Evana Network emerged amid 2015 MC USA controversies. Evana (abbreviating "evangelical Anabaptist" theology) speaks of embracing the 1995 COF but also various confessions of the Mennonite Brethren (yet another denomination) and CMC, even as it asks members to commit to requirements as "defined in our covenant" and expects congregations to belong to a Congregational Covenant.

Statements Evana embraces vary in emphasis and details. For example, the 1995 COF speaks of a "fully reliable and trustworthy" Bible even as CMC affirms Scripture as "without error in the original writings in all that they affirm." Evident here a century later are ongoing effects of Fundamentalist/Modernist controversies.

Then one could ponder Anabaptists emphasizing a Jesus manifested in social and communal ethics versus Jesus as personal savior. In *The Absent Christ: A Theology of the Empty Tomb* (Cascadia, 2020), Justin Heinzekehr describes a God "mediated to the world in and through material relations." Reviewing in *Brethren in Christ History and Life* (Aug. 2021), pastor Zachary Speidel says that for Heinzekehr, Christ's *absence* makes space for the sacred "to be inseparably bound up in ethical relationships with . . . others." But Seidel underscores Jesus' *presence*: "When I speak of 'Jesus,' I speak of my Savior, my Lord, my Friend, and my Shepherd."

THE ANABAPTIST TRADITION

* * *

When I was pastor in 2008 at Spring Mount Mennonite Church, we faced such larger dynamics but also complexities in our immediate setting. To remain viable, given the congregation's dwindling to 35-some participants, we needed to welcome persons from diverse backgrounds. Pointing in microcosm to increasing diversity of Anabaptist-Mennonitism, often growing most quickly in cultures and settings beyond North America or within the US beyond earlier ethnic and racial enclaves, eventually about half the congregation came from diverse settings. These ranged from Roman Catholic and Protestant denominations to "Nones" sometimes having no prior faith commitments.

What beliefs might we hold in common? After 11 years of wrestling with this, in my final months I preached sermons summarizing five values Anabaptist-Mennonites often emphasize while still embracing many affirmations of other Christian traditions:

The first involves "No other foundation can anyone lay than that which is laid, which is Jesus Christ" (1 Cor. 3:11). That introduces VALUE 1: *The starting point for Anabaptist-Mennonite understandings of God, the church, and all life is the New Testament and the Jesus Christ revealed in it.* If we find understandings in Scripture, church, world, or our lives that conflict with New Testament teachings about Jesus' Way, we give Jesus priority.

This is why the Sermon on the Mount is key to daily living. Jesus repeats, again and again, "You have heard that it was said . . . But I say to you . . ." Here Jesus reshapes the lives of followers—including Anabaptists—by teaching radical understandings of how God works and what God expects of us.

VALUE 2: *God's kingdom or realm comes first.* This Anabaptist-Mennonite teaching has roots in the 1500s. Back then church and state often intertwined in what is sometimes called Christendom. Being baptized as a baby into your state church made you Christian. As radicals reforming the Reformers, the Anabaptists concluded Jesus taught that infant baptism doesn't make you Christian. Rather, to be Christian is to make an adult decision to follow Jesus.

When you decide to follow, you become a citizen of God's nation. You put God's realm first. If your earthly nation, society, community, or even church asks you to violate the teachings of Christ and ways of God, you obey God.

VALUE 3: *An Anabaptist-Mennonite church is a believers church.* A believers church is made up not of people born into it but of people who have consciously decided to follow Jesus.

That decision is momentous. Only those who grasp the meaning and cost of following Jesus should be baptized, Anabaptists claimed. This was how Anabaptists, meaning "rebaptizers," as their enemies named them, came to see adult baptism as important enough to die for when Christendom entities ordered them to stop.

Although, as is evident above, this can catalyze division. The dream is that you and your co-believers will form alternative accountability structures helping you discern Jesus' way and find wisdom and courage to live it.

VALUE 4: *Anabaptist-Mennonites are committed to love and nonviolence.* We believe this because Jesus taught and modeled it, even dying on the cross and forgiving those who put him there. This means together cultivating a personal lifestyle of loving enemies and forgiving those who hurt or offend us. This has generated Mennonite contributions to conflict transformation. It means we can't in good conscience follow

Jesus *and* kill other people. So in theory (not always in practice) we don't participate in war even if the alternative is prison, as Mennonites faced in World War I, or conscientious objection, as I registered for during the Vietnam War.

VALUE 5: *Anabaptist-Mennonites embrace wholistic mission.* We share Christ's love with souls *and* bodies. The saving news of the gospel must be shared. And Jesus wants the bodies of God's children—of those blind, captive, oppressed, as he put it in Luke 4, and the "least of these," as he named them in Matthew 25—to be cherished. This means caring when injustice, racism, poverty, hunger, or nakedness befall any of God's children or creation itself and has led to such service organizations as Mennonite Disaster Service and Mennonite Central Committee.

These five values are neither exhaustive nor speak for all Anabaptist-Mennonites. Many treasures and shadows—or ways Anabaptism might correct other traditions or be corrected—await other venues (and are so far touched on in responses to Orthodoxy, Catholicism, and Lutheranism). Yet I hope I've hinted at our complex, sometimes tormented, sometimes spine-tingling history and beliefs.

Highlights of Responses from Other Christian Traditions

Five Core Values That Many Anabaptist-Mennonites Emphasize: While acknowledging the diversity of beliefs between various strands of the Anabaptist/Mennonite tradition, Michael King, our Anabaptist CP, cites five foundational values that "many" in his tradition embrace, and which elicit mixed responses from the other CPs.

Value 1: The starting point for Anabaptist-Mennonite understandings for God, the church, and all of life is the New Testament and the Jesus Christ revealed in it.

It is on the basis of this value that Anabaptists–Mennonites place special emphasis on the Sermon on the Mount. A number of the CPs point to the radical revolutionary nature of this first value since it gives primacy to the Sermon on the Mount. For example, Randall Balmer, our Anglican CP, observes that "not many people in our world turn the other cheek or believe that the weak will inherit the earth or that peacemakers are blessed."

But Wesley Granberg-Michaelson, our Reformed CP, asks whether the focus on the Sermon on the Mount "pays adequate attention to the whole of the biblical witness." He asks whether "the Hebrew scriptures [are] simply set aside when there is a possible contradiction with the New Testament," calling for a "deeper engagement with the Word of God."

I now take the liberty of sharing my reflections on the tension I perceive between the views of Balmer and Granberg-Michaelson expressed above. factoring in the response of Michael King (our Anabaptist CP) to this tension in his end-of-the month posting, which was that he was raised in a "what Jesus teaches trumps everything else" context, but as result of his being "exposed to more scholarly biblical studies," he "came to see that all of scriptures are to be engaged" (adding his "Yes" to Granberg-Michaelson's "complexifications").

First, I embrace the teaching in Matthew 5: 17 – 20 that Jesus came to fulfill the law and the prophets, not to abolish them. But I understand this fulfillment to refer to the manner in which the Old Testament writings of the prophets points Christians in New Testament times to the importance acting justly and mercifully (e.g., see Micah 6:8); especially on behalf of the poor and marginalized members of society (as strongly suggested in Matthew 25).

But my embracing that belief does not preclude my giving priority to the commitment to non-violence taught by Jesus in the Sermon on the Mount. Jesus rejects the idea that Christians sometimes need to kill other human beings to fulfill the law and the prophets.

Value 2: God's kingdom or realm comes first.

King asserts that an implication of this value is that "when you decide to follow Jesus, you become a citizen of God's nation. If your earthly nation, society, community, or even church asks you to violate the teachings of Jesus and ways of God, you obey God." The other CPs do not reflect on this assertion.

Value 3: An Anabaptist-Mennonite church is a believers church.

It is on the basis of this value that Anabaptist-Mennonites limit church membership to those who have made a conscious decision to follow Jesus; requiring that those who have been baptized in other Christian traditions need to be "re-baptized" after making this decision. This belief elicited much commentary from other CPs, especially from those within traditions that practice infant baptism, who argue against the need to be "re-baptized." No consensus was reached as to "who should be baptized and when."

Value 4: Anabaptist-Mennonites are committed to love and nonviolence.

This value elicited a number of concerns from other CPs since the majority of Christians do not embrace pacifism. For example, although our other CPs do not use the words "tragic moral choice," is it possible that "going to war" may sometimes be the "least destructive" alternative in a situation where all the alternatives for action are destructive, such as in the decision to go to war to fight the ambitions of Adolph Hitler for world domination?

The most compelling expression of concern about always precluding the use of violence was expressed by Farris Blount, our CP representing the Black Church. Calling our attention to the pivotal role that our biographies have on our position on this issue, or any issue, Farris says that "while I believe in a commitment to love and nonviolence, Black churches have often been subject to violence and **forced to fight back** in order to just survive" (emphasis mine). The looming question then is what should be the nature of that "fight"?

Value 5: Anabaptist-Mennonites embrace wholistic mission.

This value embraces a broad view of Christian mission as including BOTH an experience of personal salvation offered by Jesus Christ AND participating in the fostering of God's redemptive purposes for all of Creation (to which I would add a particular focus on addressing the needs of poor and other marginalized groups in society, as taught by Jesus—see Matthew 25).

Many of our CPs expressed enthusiastic support for this Anabaptist-Mennonite call to "wholistic mission."

Questions for Future Conversation

Q1: Do you embrace the five values that are foundational to the Anabaptist-Mennonite understanding of what it means to follow Jesus? If not, which values do you call into question and why?

Q2: What is your position on "who should be baptized and when?"

Q3: Do you believe that Christians (and everyone else) can find themselves in situations of "tragic moral choice" where all the available actions are destructive, and one must choose the "least destructive alternative?" If so, can you provide some examples? Is killing another human being in a war ever justified as a "tragic moral choice?" Can you provide other examples of what you believe to be "tragic moral choices?"

Q4: If you ever find yourself in the position where you need to "fight back in order to survive," what should be the nature of that "fight"?

Q5: What do you understand to be the relationship between the teachings of Jesus in the Sermon on the Mount and the laws and teachings of the prophets found in the Old Testament?

Grateful to Respondents for Bringing Bones to Life

Summaries, as I found when delineating five values in "Amid Complexities, Five Things Many Anabaptist-Mennonites Emphasize," leave unsettling numbers of things unsaid. So I'm grateful for conversation partners' responses; repeatedly you brought to life precisely the "bones" of those stripped-down values. Let me respond appreciatively in the order in which you each posted.

Robert Millet, there are variations in how we view and practice baptism, but yes to highlighting mature awareness of baptism's meaning: "Latter-day Saints are also emphatic about *who* should be baptized—namely, only those who are accountable and mature enough to understand why they are being baptized and why the ordinance is performed in the specific manner."

You also wondered about "a Mennonite perspective toward holy Scripture—that it is 'without error in the original writings in all that they affirm.'" Some Mennonites do hold this view, which raises complexities you point to, including what we do about Scripture's reliability without access to the original documents. I'd expect it's no accident that the 1995 *Confession of Faith* affirmed by my Mennonite Church USA denomination speaks instead of a "fully reliable and trustworthy" Bible. This is my view.

Although I'd balance your "'holy envy' in how these Christians live out their faith" with awareness of Anabaptist-Mennonite shadows, your thoughts on war and the love and forgiveness the Amish exemplify are heartwarming.

Farris Blount, you movingly put flesh on dry bones of my post. You observe that "Black churches have often been subjected to violence and forced to fight back just to survive. I wonder how we might consider the Anabaptist dedication to peace in light of the experiences of a Black Church tradition that is partially defined by the violence it has endured."

On the one hand, 1500s Anabaptists–Mennonites had to discern how to live dedicated to peace as other Christians drowned and burned them. On the other hand, and here I see a crucial difference, they didn't face centuries of systemic racism and attendant violence. As you observe, "love and nonviolence were hallmarks of Black congregations and pastors who were at the forefront of the Civil Rights Movement. To them, Jesus was love and nonviolence enfleshed and a model for how the Black Church could advocate for changes in discriminatory policies and practices." You rightly underscore:

THE ANABAPTIST TRADITION

The Black Church has often had to contend with real violence that has harmed its members. White "Christians" would don the Ku Klux Klan uniform and terrorize African Americans, burning their churches and lynching Black Americans for no apparent reason other than hatred. The American enslavement of Black people was predicated on violence; Black slaves were raped, tortured, beaten, and killed, all in the name of maintaining control of a system that saw them as the non-human other, often at the hands of self-professed Christian slaveowners.

I'm reminded that Anabaptists have pondered how to establish a "community hermeneutic" in which Scripture, the Holy Spirit, the teachings of Jesus, and given contexts form crucibles within which communities discern what God is saying in this place and time. Your concerns delineate key factors in Black communities of discernment which in turn inform any of us. I want to honor your insightful naming of "the complicated relationship that Black communities have with violence" and the validity of a question such as "How can we expect someone to remain committed to nonviolence when history demonstrates that the most violent, often in the name of God, have been the most successful and prosperous?"

Sarah Lancaster, thank you for articulating United Methodist and Anabaptist-Mennonite points of overlap and occasional differences. When I was dean of Eastern Mennonite Seminary, the second-most important student cohort was UM. To help maintain our approval to teach UM students, it was my job to report to the UM University Senate how EMS connected with the "Social Principles." If I were still dean, I'd look for ways to quote from your insights.

Christopher Gehrz, you understandably wish I had said more about Pietistism and Anabaptism. I hinted at this in describing a pastor hungry for the living presence of Christ in a book he was reviewing, but much remains unexplored. Thanks for your critical yet affirming overview of the Anabaptist-Pietist dialectic and ways you see Dale Brown offering a path forward.

David Gushee, I resonate with your sadness regarding a "dizzying array of schisms and divisions" and their causes. I also would see little reason to challenge your Baptist affirmation of a "near-total convergence"!

Wesley Granberg-Michaelson, you help us all simultaneously see areas of commonality and difference between the Reformed tradition and Anabaptism. Thank you for highlighting our mutual values *and* ways Reformed and Lutheran traditions have wrestled with persecution of Anabaptists.

You wonder if christocentrism sets the Hebrew Scriptures aside. "Isn't a deeper engagement with the whole Word of God required?" Here is a downside of brief expression of values. I *was* raised in a "what Jesus teaches trumps everything else" context. However, once exposed to more scholarly biblical studies, I came see that all of Scriptures are to be engaged. Yes to your complexifications here.

Randall Balmer, your affirmations of "those countercultural Anabaptists" are welcome. And you rightly note this "underselling":

Mr. King mentions the importance of pacifism, but I'm afraid he undersells the point. Yes, Anabaptists faced persecution and public opprobrium during World War I and the Vietnam War, but that persecution has a much longer history.... Hutterites, to take one example, fled to Russia and then to North America (especially Montana, the Dakotas, and the Prairie Provinces) to escape military conscription, and Anabaptists faced double taxation, distraint of goods, and vigilante violence because of

THE ANABAPTIST TRADITION

their refusal to participate in 18th-century military conflicts, the Seven Years' War, and the Revolutionary War.

Mark Ellingsen, you pose great questions about whether Lutheran dialectical thought can be an appropriate gospel witness. You highlight the appeal to you and yours of a countercultural witness. And you persist in having fun by "confounding the world for Jesus' sake." Then you wrap up with this captivating question:

I need to clarify whether a Mennonite congregation would even consider a sinful sleaze like me as a member (for countercultural Christian though I try to be, I am still the same selfish, concupiscent being I've always been) and whether I would have to renounce my baptism in order to join. If we can get around these issues, Mennonites and Lutherans could have a lot of fun following Jesus together.

I may fail my tradition by not delving into all the "legalities" adequately. But Mark, as one who has in prior responses highlighted Anabaptist-Mennonite struggles with faithfulness-turned-schismatic-legalism, whatever it takes, we need to have this fun!

Christina Wassell, valuable comments on baptism in Roman Catholic perspective: "Because Christ spoke so clearly on the need to be baptized as a part of the normal path of salvation (making room here for Baptism by desire or by blood) Holy Mother Church flings out her arms with this sacrament, in a sense, and accepts Christian Baptism broadly." You mention Catholic acceptance of various forms of baptism versus the "believers church" approach you experienced when told at age nine "that now that I was old enough to choose faith for myself, it was best that I be baptized *again*."

I won't respond systematically to your excellent questions, including whether sin can erase the mark of baptism or Anabaptism can honor the baptism of your age-nine self. But the possibility of falling away from Christ is present in my tradition; that's why at nine myself I was terrified I'd fall from Jesus into damnation. I draw comfort from the it's-not-all-on-you Catholic extension of grace.

Your youthful baptism: By age eight my own daughter wanted to mark following Jesus with baptism. Not ideal from a classic Anabaptist perspective. But there was genuine hunger. Her pastor's conclusion: She'd mature in understanding the import of her decision, but her clarity of conviction must be honored. After age-appropriate tutoring in the meaning of following Jesus, he baptized her. She follows on.

David Ford, you cite this 1995 Mennonite confession article: "We believe that God has **created the heavens and the earth** and all that is in them, and that God preserves and renews what has been made. All creation has its source outside itself and belongs to the creator. The world has been created good because God is good and provides all that is needed for life." You say:

> [T]his tremendously positive, creation-affirming statement could well be the basis upon which Anabaptists and Mennonites might develop a sacramental understanding of the material world and all of creation—a view that would be in accord with the sacramental understanding of all of the material realm that the Orthodox Church has always held from the very beginning.

You open my tradition to me in ways I hadn't thought of!

J. Terry Todd, your hints at possible responses to your questions anticipate how I might answer. I concur: At least potentially for Mennonites resistance is witness. Another example:

THE ANABAPTIST TRADITION

Herald Press has issued many editions of the *More with Less Cookbook*, by Doris Janzen. Long before climate change hit headlines, Janzen taught millions about eating that resists harming the planet.

I responded more fully on your post to your wondering about "*spiritual* and *emotional* violence at work among these peacemakers." But I resonate, hence why most of my postings reference Mennonite shadows. I also resonate with your seeing overlap between Mennonite and Pentecostal shadows and your take on schismatic splitting.

V. THE ANGLICAN TRADITION
RANDALL BALMER

Following Jesus along the Canterbury Trail

I have two semi-flippant responses when people ask me how I, reared as an evangelical, became an Episcopalian and, in 2006, an Episcopal priest. My father was a pastor for forty years in the Evangelical Free Church; I honor both his ministry and his memory, and on the whole I'm grateful for my upbringing within the evangelical subculture, if for no other reason than that it helped to form my character by giving me something to push against. The Episcopal Church, however, couldn't be farther removed from my childhood experience of faith; the first time I saw a cleric in a purple shirt, for example, I thought it was simply bad taste. Evangelicalism is part of my DNA, and much of my scholarship over the past several decades has sought to acquaint evangelicals with their own laudable history of concern for those on the margins and thereby summon evangelicals back from their errant ways; that is, the Faustian bargain they made with the far-right reaches of the Republican Party beginning in 1980. (You can judge for yourself how successful I've been in those efforts!)

Despite my appreciation for the religious formation of my childhood, I began to yearn for something deeper, which brings me to the two explanations for my spiritual pilgrimage: First, becoming an Episcopalian, I say, was a reaction to the aesthetic deprivation of my childhood. That's a bit of an overstatement, but it also contains an element of truth. The second explanation is that I grew weary of the evangelical cult of novelty, where the directive every week was "Let's try something new!" This penchant for innovation has undeniably fueled the growth of evangelicalism throughout American history—evangelicals know almost instinctively how to speak the idiom of the culture, whether it be the open-air preaching of George Whitefield and other itinerants during the Great Awakening, the circuit riders and the colporteurs of the nineteenth century, the urban revivalists of the twentieth century, or the suburban megachurches of recent vintage.

As a historian, however, I wanted to respond, "No, let's try something old instead." Add to all that a sprinkling of Anglophilia (I initially intended to study British history in graduate school), and by the time I wandered into Trinity Church, in Princeton, New Jersey, I felt as though I had come home. I loved the music, and the liturgy suggested a connectedness to the past, to the "communion of the saints." Even the space itself told me that something important transpired there. I wasn't sure at the time what it was, but it seemed sacred to me and very much unlike the cavernous and (yes, I'll say it) soulless spaces all too typical of evangelicalism.

I love the cadences of the *Book of Common Prayer*, the reverence of the liturgy, the soaring descants of the Anglican musical tradition, and prayers that typically do not include the phrase, "Lord, we jus' wanna." I've come to regard the Episcopal Church, along with museums, symphonies, and the natural world, as one of the few remaining repositories of beauty in this life.

And, most important, a focus on the sacraments, especially Holy Communion. As a priest, I intentionally keep my sermons short because the homily is merely a stop on the way to the Eucharist, the culmination of the liturgy. I don't want in any way to detract from the "main event," the real presence of Jesus in the bread and wine of Holy Communion.

I'm well aware of the fact that, six paragraphs into this discursus, I've yet to talk explicitly about theology in the Anglican tradition. The quick explanation is that I'm a historian, not a theologian. But the larger reason is that, although Anglicanism has its share of good theologians as well as the *Thirty-nine Articles*, doctrine does not lie at the core of Anglican or Episcopal identity (the Anglican Church in the United States reconfigured itself as the Episcopal Church in 1789, following the American Revolution, though it remains part of the worldwide Anglican Communion).

The focus of Anglican identity is worship and sacraments and liturgy, especially as encoded in the *Book of Common Prayer*. That is what holds us together as followers of Jesus. Anglicans and Episcopalians can—and do—disagree on many things, but we find common ground in the Prayer Book. The Episcopal Church is by no means perfect; all institutions are human constructs, and they are remarkably poor vessels for piety. But this is my venue for following Jesus.

This de-emphasis of theology exposes us to the charge of latitudinarianism, a criticism that is not entirely unfounded. But a focus on liturgy and the mysteries of the sacraments also shields us from what I will call the cult of Enlightenment Rationalism, especially the logic choppers who slice and dice and reduce the faith into tidy theological categories. The obsession with doctrinal precisionism, such as what I encountered at my evangelical seminary, is one of the factors that pointed me beyond evangelicalism and, eventually, to the Episcopal Church. My seminary professors had it all figured out, with fancy apologetic schemes and answers to every theological contingency. But where is the mystery of faith?

I've come to see that doubt is not the antithesis of faith; it is an essential component of faith. Besides, if we've got it all figured out, what need is there for faith? My favorite passage in the New Testament is the anguished cry from the father of a young child. "Lord, I believe," he tells Jesus, "help my unbelief!"

I am drawn to the Episcopal Church in part because I refuse to allow the canons of Enlightenment Rationalism to serve as the final arbiter of truth. I elect to live in an enchanted universe where there are forces at play that I cannot begin to understand, much less explain—not least of which is the mystery of the real presence of Christ in the Eucharist.

In describing my religious pilgrimage, I'm well aware that I come off as something of a cliché—an evangelical kid who trots off to college, acquires some education and decides that he must leave behind the faith of his childhood. It's a phenomenon that one of my mentors, Mark Noll, long ago characterized as "Evangelicals on the Canterbury Trail." For many of these evangelical pilgrims, the next steps along the pathway are Roman Catholicism and then Eastern Orthodoxy.

At the risk of sounding defensive, I don't believe I fit that cliché, at least not entirely. First, I have not totally given up on evangelicalism (though I've been sorely tempted many times in recent years, most acutely following the 2016 election).

Second, although I've been encouraged to do so by people

ranging from my wife to the bishop who ordained me, Jeffrey Steenson, one of my oldest friends who himself decamped to Rome, I don't think I could ever "swim the Tiber" to Roman Catholicism. The issue for me is what I take to be a flawed interpretation of Matthew 16, where Jesus declares that his church would be built upon Peter, "the rock." Rather than pointing to the primacy of Peter (who may or may not have been the first bishop of Rome), this passage, I believe, is one of the few attempts at humor—or irony at least—in the New Testament. Peter, as we know, was anything but solid. He was dithering and spineless, insisting that he would never disavow Jesus but caving to pressure from a young girl. And when Peter tried to walk on the Sea of Galilee, he took his eyes off Jesus and sank beneath the waves—like a rock.

Far from designating Peter as first among equals, let alone justifying papal infallibility, the beauty of this passage lies in the fact that Jesus was willing to entrust the church, his entire earthly legacy, to flawed human beings like Peter—and, by extension, to flawed beings like you and me. I mean no disrespect to my Roman Catholic friends, and I find much to admire about Roman Catholicism, but papal infallibility is a bridge too far—even one constructed over the Tiber.

For that reason, I'll be content to follow Jesus along the Canterbury Trail.

Highlights of Responses from Other Christian Traditions

FOLLOWING JESUS WITHOUT ALL THE ANSWERS: Randall Balmer, our Anglican CP, reports on the tension he experienced in his pilgrimage from Evangelicalism to the Episcopal tradition between the Anglican focus on worship and the sacraments, especially as encoded in the *Book of Common Prayer* and the obsession with "doctrinal precision" that he was exposed to in his seminary education under Evangelical auspices. His eventual choice to follow Jesus within the Episcopal tradition was informed by three factors: (1) His strong aesthetic sense and his appreciation of the Episcopal Church as "one of the few remaining repositories of beauty in this life"; (2) The fact that he "grew weary of the of the evangelical cult of novelty, where the directive every week was 'Let's try something new!'" (as an historian, Balmer prefers to say "No, let's try something old instead"); and (3) His rejection of the quest for doctrinal precision within Evangelicalism as not taking into the account the "mystery of faith" ("I elect to live in an enchanted universe where there are forces at play that I cannot begin to understand, much less explain").

Balmer's rejection of the quest for doctrinal precision struck a chord with a number of the other CPs. For example, Chris Gehrz, our Pietist CP, stresses the importance of Christians "seeking together after Jesus Christ as people of faith and doubt; inhabitants of what Randall aptly calls an 'enchanted universe,' whose mysteries a primarily intellectual faith 'cannot begin to understand, much less explain.'"

But Christina Wassell, our Catholic CP, demurs, reporting that her pilgrimage from Anglicanism to the Roman Catholic Church was informed by her belief that "some of the uncertainty that is just a part of being Anglican" provided too much "room" for disagreement ("While I surely appreciate the mystery of the faith, the degree of diversity what a priest or a member of the church might believe on a given topic felt too roomy"). This concern raises the thorny issue as to whether there are limits (boundaries) to the diversity of Christian beliefs, both within and across Christian traditions.

Possible Limits on the Diversity of

Christian Beliefs about What it Means to Follow Jesus?

A number of our CPs point us toward the importance of first understanding the "source" of diversity in Christian beliefs among those equally committed to following Jesus. Our differences in beliefs are significantly affected by "who we are," which includes our personality traits, the particularities of our social location, such as our gender, or race or ethnicity, our socio-economic status and our sexual orientation, and our personal biographies (the stories of our lives). Terry Todd, our Pentecostal CP, summarizes this nicely when he asserts that "The approach to the question [of what it means to follow Jesus within a given Christian tradition] requires a deep dive into the context and the lives of those within the traditions."

Our CPs do not reach any consensus as to the drawing of "red lines" (setting boundaries) as to what are acceptable positions for Christians in any tradition to hold relative to some contentious issues, especially noting the strong disagreements that presently pervade many Christian traditions regarding human sexuality issues such as same-sex marriage.

My own reflection on this challenging issue is informed by the position taken by Roger Olson in his book *Reformed and Always Reforming*, in which he proposes a paradigm for doing theology that calls for a centered set of Christian beliefs rather than a bounded set. This paradigm suggests that the current preoccupation with establishing firm boundaries to decide who is inside and who is outside the Christian fold should be replaced by who is near the center and who is moving away from the center, with, in my estimation, the "center" being Jesus Christ.

Questions for Future Conversation

Q1: What is your assessment of the suggestion that Christians need to learn to faithfully follow Jesus without "having all the answers"? If that is correct, how do you proceed with making day-to-day decisions on how to live?

Q2: Do you agree with the assertion that your beliefs are influenced by "who you are"? If you disagree, why?

Q3: What limits (boundaries) would you draw, if any, as to acceptable beliefs for Christians to hold? Why?

Q4: What do you think of Roger Olson's proposal that rather than setting boundaries as to who is a Christian or not on the basis of their particular beliefs, we should ask "who is near the center [Jesus Christ] and who is moving away from the center"? If you agree with Olson, what are the signs of being near the center or moving away from the center?

Q5: What do you think of a proposal that what "holds us together" (within or across Christian traditions) is EITHER shared practices of worship OR agreement on doctrinal issues? If you think this is a false choice (it is both/and, not either/or), explain yourself.

Q6: The experiences of a number of our CPs point to the importance of exposing oneself to the differing beliefs of those embedded in Christian traditions other than one's own tradition. What is the extent of your exposure to such "theological otherness"? If you have sought such exposure, how have you found it to be helpful? If you have not had such exposure, why not?

Response to Anglican/Episcopal Comments

I've often said that a scholar can receive no greater compliment than to have others interact seriously with his ideas. I thank all of you for your thoughtful comments, and although I won't be able to respond to every point (due to limitations on space and your patience), I shall try to address at least something from each post.

ORTHODOX: I thank David Ford for his observations about the affinities between Anglicanism and Orthodoxy, in part because of a rejection of scholasticism and a mutual suspicion of papal infallibility. Although I have reservations about ecumenism in general, I agree that our two traditions have much in common, something I tried to argue when I was (briefly) a member of the Episcopal Church delegation on ecumenical relations. Yes, I'm sure it's true that some in the Anglican tradition deny the bodily resurrection of Jesus (a position I find truly regrettable, even heretical), but to foreswear the possibility of intercommunion because of the ordination of women or the acceptance of those with alternate sexual identities is, in my view, both short-sighted and not consonant with the teaching and the demeanor of Jesus that we find in the New Testament.

ROMAN CATHOLIC: Some of my comments in the preceding paragraph apply here as well, and I'm very aware that papal infallibility has been invoked sparingly since the doctrine was devised during the First Vatican Council. That does not diminish its hubris. As for being "niggled" by the origins of Anglicanism (because Henry VIII wanted a divorce), sure, I wish I could point to more noble beginnings. But the formation of the Church of England underscores the flawed and very human character of institutions—not unlike Peter himself and the Roman Catholic Church—and all the more reason that those of us who follow Jesus should strike a pose of humility rather than grandiosity when it comes to claims of truth or supremacy. As St. Paul says, "we know in part, and we prophesy in part" (1 Corinthians 13:9). Ms. Wassell raises the issue of politics, particularly surrounding the abortion issue. I have no reason to question the sincerity of many of those who line up in the antiabortion camp—including, I have no doubt, Ms. Wassell herself—but the irrefutable fact remains that the Religious Right mobilized in the 1970s in defense of racial segregation in evangelical institutions, not in response to *Roe v. Wade*. And it's not simply a matter of shrugging this off by professing to judge a tree by its fruit. My sense as a historian is that unacknowledged and unrepented racism tends to fester, as we saw in 2016 when the Religious Right finally abandoned the pretense that theirs was a movement concerned with "family values" and 81 percent of white evangelicals supported Donald Trump. (Here is an instance where the tree and its fruits metaphor might actually be instructive, though it leads to a far different conclusion from the one Ms. Wassell favors.) Opposition to abortion may be a worthy crusade. (I believe it is, by the way, although I think it should be addressed as a *moral* issue, not a *legal* issue. Put another way, I have no interest in making abortion illegal; I would like to make it unthinkable.) But it is also undeniable that a singular focus on abortion has distorted our approach to other, equally important, matters. As I asked in an earlier posting, in what moral universe do the Catholic bishops consider censuring Joe Biden, a devout Catholic, while heaping praise on Donald Trump?

LUTHERAN: I love Mark Ellingsen's invocation of the communion of the saints, one of my favorite phrases from the Nicene Creed. That sense of connectedness both to the past as well as to fellow (contemporary) believers is compelling—and comforting. Mr. Ellingsen's comments also prompt me to wonder if there is indeed a correlation between a liturgical focus and a (healthy) suspicion of too strong a reliance on reason. And yes—of course!—justification by grace, which entails freedom from the law. Finally, in response to the final question: "But is there a place for the Lutheran emphasis on freedom and spontaneity in Anglican circles (especially as we celebrate the liturgy together)?" I'd sure like to think so, and it is certainly true that alternate forms and liturgies are used extensively, depending on the parish. At the same time, Episcopalians, "God's frozen chosen," are not often known for spontaneity!

ANABAPTIST: I appreciate Michael King's "catholic" tastes when it comes to spirituality; Frederick Buechner has long been a favorite of mine, along with the inimitable Anne Lamott. And I love the fact that Mr. King, having ranged far afield, has chosen fully to inhabit his own Anabaptist tradition. I think that's admirable, and I honor it. (I've tried to do the same, and I think to some extent I've succeeded, but failing to speak out against the execrable politics to which many evangelicals have succumbed would, I believe, constitute moral cowardice.)

REFORMED TRADITION: My friend (and neighbor) Wes Granberg-Michaelson raises an important point: The Reformers' break with Roman Catholicism necessitated the formulation of various creeds so that these breakaway movements could "clarify what they believed" and "provide a definitive rational statement of theological convictions." Having rejected the twin bases of authority that underlie the Roman Catholic Church, Scripture and tradition, Reformers had to devise their own formulae based on their reading of the Bible. This led inevitably to the splintering of Protestantism because the Bible, as we know, admits of many interpretations. I'm also heartened to hear that many congregations in the Reformed tradition are paying more attention to the Lord's Supper. (I was aware of this anecdotally, but Mr. Granberg-Michaelson is an authoritative source.) Could the *Book of Common Prayer* have overcome apartheid? A fair question, and one that probably cannot be answered definitively. But it is undeniably the case that an Anglican archbishop (and lover of the *Book of Common Prayer*), the late Desmond Tutu, certainly contributed mightily to that struggle.

BAPTIST: Another dear and admired friend, David Gushee, has recounted his own flirtation with the Episcopal Church, but he, like Michael King, returned to his Baptist roots. (What is it about you Baptists!) Mr. Gushee wonders "whether there is enough shared substance for the discipleship journey" within the Anglican tradition. He goes on to say that the primacy of liturgy over theology (a point I may have oversold) has not spared Anglicans/Episcopalians from schism. A fair argument, though I'm not sure that doctrinal uniformity would have forestalled that development. Mr. Gushee points out the relative absence of Anglican contributions to his field, Christian Ethics. Yes, I suppose that's true, and I'm hard-pressed for an explanation. (It's been a long time since I was Paul Ramsey's TA in his Christian Ethics classes at Princeton, and I haven't kept up with the field; the only Anglican reading I can recall was a pamphlet on the issue of divorce and remarriage.) Thank you, finally, for acknowledging the capaciousness of the Anglican tradition, and yes, there is "something biblical about that."

PIETISM: I'm gratified to hear that my essay resonated with Christopher Gehrz, and we have yet another testimonial to the lure of the Anglican tradition—the Choral Eucharist, Evensong, Epiphany Carols, and worship "in the beauty of holiness." I love Mr. Gehrz's invocation of the followers of Jesus as a "people of faith and doubt" as well as Pietism's commitment "to seek a via media around the Reformation's most destructive dead ends, that Pietists can certainly celebrate in

THE ANGLICAN TRADITION

Anglicanism." And yes, I also believe that diverse pathways of faith lead to similar ends. Amen.

WESLEYAN: I thank Sarah Lancaster for reminding us of the close historical ties between Anglicanism and Methodism. The Wesleys' Methodism, with its emphasis on warm-hearted piety, was part of a broader eighteenth-century reaction against scholasticism, a movement that encompassed Continental Pietism, Quietism among Roman Catholics, and even Hasidism among Jews. And yes, it is probably true that the Methodist–Episcopal divide developed because the latter "felt a greater need for maintaining proper liturgy and sacraments," although the evangelical in me certainly agrees that personal experience is more important than "tidy theological categories." You have my sympathy as a denomination for the current contestation over LGBTQ++ issues. I fervently hope before I pass on to my reward to see some denomination threaten to split over how well they are fulfilling Jesus' injunction to love their neighbors and care for "the least of these." Now that would be a fight worth waging!

BLACK CHURCH: Farris Blount heralds the "creative freedom" in a tradition not defined principally by doctrine, but he wonders "to what degree such an openness can be detrimental to those who are new to the Anglican tradition, as there is no orienting theological structure to help them make sense of their faith in and commitment to Jesus." That may be true (though it wasn't for me), but I would emphatically contest Mr. Blount's assertion that the *Book of Common Prayer* doesn't contain "the actual words or instructions" of Jesus. To the contrary, the Prayer Book brims with the words and the teachings of Jesus, and one of my revelations when I began attending an Episcopal church was that each service contained a whole lot more reading of Scripture than I heard in evangelical churches. I quite agree that too often Christians, evangelicals especially, have elevated the words of Paul over the words and the example of Jesus. I've often said that you can construct a pretty reliable taxonomy of Christian denominations by tracking which portions of the Bible they gravitate to. For evangelicals, it tends to be the Pauline epistles—most likely because Paul is a moralist, and he tells them what to do. But if you believe (as I do) that Jesus is the "*word* of God" (see John 1), then it seems to me that the Gospels merit greater attention.

LATTER-DAY SAINTS: First, let's agree that my friend Robert Millet crafted by far the best title in this round of postings: "From the Sawdust Trail to the Canterbury Trail." Brilliant! Mr. Millet was kind enough to refer to some of my earlier writings, and to do so with appreciation, even suggesting that they have helped him in his commendable efforts to forge new understandings between evangelicals and Latter-day Saints. At first blush, I find Boyd Packer's reflections on the importance of doctrine quite compelling: "The study of the doctrines of the gospel will improve behavior quicker than a study of behavior will improve behavior." But as I reflect further, I'm not certain that I agree that the purpose of doctrine is to regulate behavior. That sounds a bit too much like works-righteousness to me.

PENTECOSTALISM: As someone who is afflicted with the hobgoblin of consistency, I know that I should address my colleague J. Terry Todd with an honorific, "Mr. Todd," just as I have with others in this thread. But I'm not sure I can do so. Terry and I go way back (longer than either of us cares to tally), and he is one of my favorite people on the planet. So, here goes . . . Terry opens with a poignant and heartrending account of Christopher Ssenyonjo, an Anglican bishop in Uganda who was barred and banished from the Church of Uganda for his advocacy of LGBTQ++ rights. Terry follows this story with a simple, powerful sentence: "Ssenyonjo paid a heavy price for following Jesus." He proceeds to point out that the worldwide Anglican communion is plagued by divisions and saddled with an imperial and colonialist past. "Of all the traditions we've considered so far," Terry writes, "it's probably the Anglicans who are most beset by their imperial and colonialist heritage, which has shaped churches of the Anglican Communion in ways difficult to untangle." I think Roman Catholicism probably merits a shout-out on those grounds as well, but I take the point. Terry recalls fondly, as do I, our visit to Church of the King (later, Christ the King) parish in Valdosta, Georgia. This was an erstwhile Assemblies of God congregation that, through the influence of a young minister, Stan White (sadly, recently deceased), found its way to the Episcopal Church, all the while maintaining its Pentecostal enthusiasm. I was present on Easter Sunday, 1990, when more than two hundred congregants were confirmed into the Episcopal Church by five bishops. "Midway through 'Sing unto the Lord a New Song,'" I wrote at the time, "Church of the King looked more like Tuesday night aerobics class than Easter Sunday in an Episcopal parish." I loved that place for its receptivity to the Holy Spirit, and even more so when Terry and I returned there to film the *Mine Eyes Have Seen the Glory* documentary. So yes, I certainly feel at home in the evangelical quadrant of Anglican life.

Once again, my thanks to all of you for your thoughtful comments.

VI. The Reformed Tradition
Wesley Granberg-Michaelson

From Guilt to Grace to Gratitude

I adopted the Reformed tradition. I wasn't raised as a "child of the covenant," wasn't baptized as an infant, and never heard of the Heidelberg Catechism as a young person in church. It became my choice, or, as some Reformed theologians might say, it chose me.

American, white evangelicalism was the birthplace of my journey to faithfully following Jesus. It started young, not at the baptismal font, but in the kitchen of our home, through a conversation with my mother when I was 4½ years old. As I asked questions about God and heaven, my attentive mother replied by explaining the way of salvation. I could ask Jesus to come into my heart. Did I want to do that?

We had an appointment to see our dentist, Dr. Cartright. I asked my mother if I could accept Jesus after going to the dentist. She hesitated and explained that Jesus could come again while I was having my teeth examined. So I didn't delay and said a prayer accepting Jesus Christ as my personal Savior.

This evangelical subculture was my home, shaping my theology and worldview. My grandfather was a friend of Billy Graham. The bulletin of the church where I was raised had the words "Evangelical, Independent, and Nondenominational" prominently printed on its cover.

Young Life, an evangelical parachurch outreach to high school students, provided an avenue that started to expand my horizons of faith. It was joyful, relational, and relevant. To my parents' chagrin, my Young Life leader suggested I attend Hope College in Holland, Michigan, rather than Wheaton College. Doing so was probably the only major act of rebellion in my adolescence.

In the classrooms and chapel of Hope, a college of the Reformed Church in America, I first learned and experienced some of the distinctives of the Reformed tradition. It was more absorption, and certainly not indoctrination. Two things, upon reflection, stand out: 1) Grace comes solely as God's initiative, as pure gift. Faith is never an achievement or personal accomplishment. 2) Following Jesus can't remain individualized. It's more than "Jesus and me." It involves God and the world. That means all aspects of life and culture—science, politics, economics, art, history—are understood wholistically through the framework of faith and the sovereignty of God. This is often termed a "Reformed world and life view."

It took years more in my journey before I was ordained as a Minister of Word and Sacrament in the Reformed Church in America. But those perspectives about grace, God, and the world—which I believe are central to the Reformed tradition—have remained with me to this day as I continue to try to faithfully follow Jesus.

Beyond the core of the Reformation—grace alone, the Word alone, and faith alone—are further distinctives to being Reformed. These can also become problematic at times, often generating stereotypes about Reformed Christians.

1. The Reformed Tradition is Confessional

Relying on the Word requires clarity about what it means. Confessions do so, written relevant to historical contexts but carrying enduring truths. These words matter, formulating beliefs that become the basis for belonging. Most are from the sixteenth and seventeenth centuries. But a striking recent example is the Belhar Confession, written in response to apartheid in South Africa but communicating enduring truths about reconciliation, justice, and unity that have gained wider receptivity in parts of the Reformed world.

Yet there are dangers. Focusing on defining faith by correct propositions can imprison belief in rationalism and mistake "correct" thoughts for faithful practice. Faith then becomes detached from the whole person, and spiritual experience is suspect, subjugated to right thinking. In the recent years of my journey, I've placed more stress on practices, such as pilgrimage, which were largely rejected by the Reformers. My time on the Camino de Santiago and other paths unfolding from my contemplative journey have persuaded me that while what we think and confess carries importance, in the end we walk our way into faith.

2. The Reformed Tradition is Covenantal

When an infant is baptized in a Reformed (or other) congregation, theological critics will complain that he or she has no choice in the matter. But that is precisely the point. Christian faith is carried communally; it's personal but not individualistic. A Christian community's covenantal promises can be a vehicle for the initiative of God's grace. As a counterpoint to the hyper-individualism of modern Western culture, this seems both theologically mature and sociologically honest. So, I don't regard my prayer in the kitchen as an autonomous, individual act of free will, but as part of a mysterious movement of grace transmitted imperfectly but certainly through covenantal relationships of love. Believing and belonging are intertwined and not always sequential.

But covenant can breed exclusivity and corporate self-righteousness. It was a temptation faced both by the people of Israel and by those in Reformed communities throughout history to this day. My theological response is that the framework of God's covenantal grace keeps expanding, relentlessly and inclusively, as seen in Jesus. God's covenant is extended through God's unconditional initiative, but its boundaries are permeable, fluid, and unexpected. It's a centered set, not a bounded set.

3. The Reformed Tradition proclaims that the world belongs to God

The evangelical culture that shaped my early years contended that we were saved from the world, both eternally and through daily measures to resist its contaminating influences. The Reformed tradition stresses that all in the world is intended to be redeemed and brought under God's sovereignty. In its best expressions, this overcomes the dualism between body and soul, nature and grace, secular and sacred. It's an invitation to creative engagement between faith and culture, art, politics, science, economics, etc.

Yet at times the results of Reformed interaction with culture have been disastrous. I recall visiting the Elmina slave castle on coast of Ghana. On the main floor I entered the chapel built by Dutch Reformed Christians engaged in this trade, where they worshiped and sang Psalms, extolling God's blessings. On the floor directly below, those captured were ruthlessly held in prison dungeons, awaiting transfer to slave ships. Dualism reigned supreme. Throughout history, various Reformed communities have justified slavery, apartheid, white patriarchy, and more. In the current rhetoric of white nationalism, one can hear echoes of similar racist, religious sentiments. Applying faith to all of life must come with a ruthless critique of how we are prone to use faith to justify our preexisting conditions of power and privilege with their oppressive effects.

4. The Reformed Tradition takes sin very seriously

"Total depravity" is often the starting point for classic Reformed theology. Even the Heidelberg Catechism, frequently praised for its more winsome spirit, answers Question Five by stating, "by nature I am prone to hate God and my neighbor." One can be grateful that the Reformed tradition refuses to see the world through a naïve, superficial lens and confronts the empirical evidence of its harsh realities. Yet, it seems ironic that a thoroughly negative anthropology should be cited as a theological virtue.

In fact, the term "total depravity" appears nowhere in any of the classic Reformed confessions, although its sentiments are found. But both Reformed theology and practice often get stuck in this rut. Guilt weighs heavily and persistently. At its best, the Reformed journey is described as a movement from guilt to grace to gratitude. It's an inviting pathway. The challenge, however, is that when you begin in so deep a hole, it can take a lifetime to comprehend grace and live out of gratitude, and sometimes that's not enough. When I sit with my two grandchildren on my lap, my Reformed theology gets undone. The last thing in the world I want them to hear about is total depravity. Rather, I want them to begin knowing how much they are loved and that in their inner being, they carry the image of God.

5. The Reformed Tradition is ecumenical

It's not surprising that many global leaders of the modern ecumenical movement, like W. A. Visser 't Hooft (the first WCC general secretary), Eugene Carson Blake, Henrick Kraemer, Lesslie Newbigin, and several others came from the Reformed tradition. John Calvin argued that no church was perfect, and in 1560 he proposed "a free and universal council to put an end to the divisions of Christendom." He would even "cross ten seas . . . in order to unite widely severed Churches." Believing that no church can be perfectly pure serves as a vulnerable and open starting point for ecumenism.

Regrettably, for more than four centuries of the Reformed tradition's history, Calvin's passion for church unity has been spurned. Reformed and Presbyterian churches are notorious for continual successions and divisions from one another, usually over finer points of doctrine or else various ethical issues (membership in the Freemasons, divorce, same gender relationships, etc.) that can hardly be regarded as foundational to faith in Jesus Christ. Nevertheless, Reformed ecclesiology provides a fruitful opening for addressing the shameful, sinful reality of over 45,000 separate denominations in today's world.

These major points summarize how much of the global Reformed community, numbering about 80 million Christians, seek to faithfully follow Jesus. Of course, there is wide variety and difference. In the end, this tradition insists that we are held by God's uncontrollable grace and that God invites us as disciples of Christ to serve and act out of gratitude for the sake of a world so loved by God.

Highlights of Responses from Other Christian Traditions

It's More Than "Jesus and Me": Wesley Granberg-Michaelson proposes five foci of the Reformed tradition, one of which is that *The Reformed tradition proclaims that the world belongs to God.* Based on my 29 years of immersion in the Reformed tradition, I believe that this focus is the most compelling. It embraces a broad view of God's redemptive purposes, extending beyond "personal salvation" ("Jesus and me"), as important as that is, to including God's wish to redeem all aspects of life and culture (e.g., science, politics, economics art).

The other four foci proposed by Granberg-Michaelson are that the Reformed tradition is Confessional and Covenantal, takes sin very seriously, and is ecumenical.

The other eleven CPs generally applaud the five foci of the Reformed tradition pointed out by Granberg-Michaelson. But they also point to possible misuses of each of these foci, echoing Granberg-Michaelson's own expressions of concern (in the quotations that follow).

WHEN GOOD THINGS GO BAD: At the same time that the other CPs generally applaud each of the five foci of the Reformed tradition enumerated by Granberg-Michaelson, they share his concerns that in practice some of these good things have gone bad, as follows:

Granberg-Michaelson proposes that *The Reformed tradition is Confessional,* embracing a commitment to historical statements issued by the tradition, mostly in the sixteenth and seventeenth centuries.

BUT "Focusing on defining faith by correct propositions can imprison belief in rationalism and mistake 'correct' thoughts for faithful practice."

Wesley G-M also proposes that *The Reformed traditional is Covenantal,* believing, as "a counterpoint to the hyper-individualism of modern Western culture," that "Christian faith is carried communally; it's personal but not individualistic."

BUT this emphasis on community can "breed exclusivity and corporate self-righteousness."

As already pointed out, Wesley G-M also asserts that *The Reformed tradition proclaims that the world belongs to God,* proclaiming that "all in the world is intended to be redeemed and brought under God's sovereignty."

BUT "at times the results of Reformed interaction with culture have been disastrous" ("Throughout history, various Reformed communities have justified slavery, apartheid, white supremacy").

Wesley G-M asserts that *The Reformed tradition takes sin very seriously,* even though the term "total depravity" appears nowhere in any of the classic Reformed confessions.

BUT even though "total depravity" is not officially taught in the classical Reformed confessions, "Reformed theology and practice often get stuck in this rut. Guilt weighs heavily and persistently," suggesting that what is needed is "a movement from guilt to grace to gratitude."

Finally, Wesley G-M asserts that *The Reformed tradition is ecumenical,* based on a belief that "no church can be perfectly pure," and this serves as "a vulnerable starting point for ecumenism."

BUT "Reformed and Presbyterian churches are notorious for continual successions and divisions from one another." And, if these divisions prevent conversation among those having strong disagreements within the Reformed tradition, how can one expect such divisions to dissipate when other traditions are brought together into an ecumenical conversation?

These concerns expressed by Granberg-Michaelson and other CPs will lead to a series of questions in the next section.

Questions for Future Conversation

Q1: What is your assessment of each of the five foci for the Reformed tradition proposed by Wesley Granberg-Michaelson? If you disagree with any of these foci, what is the nature of your disagreement, and what would you propose as your alternative position?

Q2: What do you believe can be done to avoid, or at least minimize, the destructive effects of what Granberg-Michaelsom suggests can "go wrong" with each of the five Reformed foci that he presents?

Q3: In his end-of-the-month response to the mid-month reflections from the other CPs, Granberg-Michaelson reaffirms his belief that "following Jesus does have a personal dimension that goes beyond the intellect," adding that "The Reformed tradition stands in continual need to develop and deepen its forms of spiritual practice that reach the soul as well as the mind." What kinds of spiritual practices do you believe best "reach the soul"?

Q4: The concerns expressed by a number of the other CPs regarding "total depravity" led Granberg-Michaelson to conclude that "There's a deep dialogue to be had around the nature of sin and the pathways of grace within the human personality." What position would you take in such a dialogue? Why?

Q5: The Reformed position that "all in the world is intended to be redeemed by God and brought under God's sovereignty" leaves unanswered two important questions. First, what is the meaning of "God's sovereignty"? Second, what is the nature of "God's power," and is there a tension between God's love and God's power? What are your thoughts about these unanswered questions?

Q6: Probing further into the Q5 questions, there appears to be a significant difference between the prevalent view in American culture that exerting "power" means "being in control," and the manner in which Jesus "gave up control" in his life and teachings, exemplifying a different kind of "power," the "power of love." What do you make of this possible distinction?

Opening Doors

Ecumenical dialogue, at its best, should prompt each of us to examine more critically and reflectively our own tradition in response to the faithful sharing of another's witness of faith from his or her tradition. That's one way in which the Spirit works to renew the understanding and living of our faith, and to uncover the unity of the Body of Christ. That unity already exists but is hidden and repressed by pride, corporate self-righteousness, fear, and spiritual insecurity. Living encounters open space for this work of the Spirit.

I'm encouraged and humbled by how this space has been opened thus far in our interchanges through Respectful Conversations. In several responses to my sharing last month of following Jesus from the Reformed tradition, others have probed depths in their traditions in ways that I've found illuminating. Doors for important connections have been found and begun to open.

J. Terry Todd, last in the sequence of responses, offers the first question: "Who Speaks for the Reformed tradition?" That gets raised by Randall Balmer, David Gushee, and Christopher Gehrz, who all wonder, in different ways, how various conservative evangelicals from different backgrounds seem drawn to forms of Calvinism. I'm puzzled as well. In part it must be a need for tight rational consistency in a persuasive, closed system of theological doctrine, as Balmer suggests. But their authoritarian and, frankly, white masculine version of a rigid Calvinism is not what draws me and millions of Christians around the world to the Reformed tradition.

The World Communion of Reformed Churches, comprised of 230 Calvinist denominations with 80 million members around the world, whose President, Rev. Najla Kassab, is a female Presbyterian pastor from Lebanon, places its focus on being "called to communion and committed to justice." Their global public profile and Reformed witness are starkly different from the "young, restless new Calvinists" that shape the popular stereotype identified by Balmer and Gushee. In truth, diverse and divergent voices try to speak for the Reformed tradition; our differences, as Gushee suggests, stem more from non-Reformed tensions in the culture.

I'm struck by how David Ford and Michael King place an emphasis on the experience of children in their responses. Ford provides a beautiful, compelling picture of the Divine Liturgy in Orthodoxy, with a child's perspective. Having participated in several experiences of Orthodox worship in my ecumenical experience, I can underscore how Ford's description captures its rich sensory and emotive qualities, bathed in a spirituality that illumines its theology. All this is a stark contrast to many forms of Reformed worship which gravitate only toward words interpreting the Word.

Orthodoxy's practice regarding children and the Eucharist, as Ford describes, finds agreement with my own understanding of covenantal theology. I find no compelling reason to justify separating the sacrament of baptism from participation in the Eucharist, at any age. Even in traditions like King's, which do not practice infant baptism, the covenant community can serve as a powerful countercultural reality against the prevailing individualism that dominates our culture and infects churches from all our traditions, as he demonstrates.

Farris Blount III presents a critique and nuanced view of covenant, however, from the experience of the Black Church that carries deep insight and power. Particularly when involving the victims of trauma and violence, he stresses that covenant needs to be continually reappraised, and I agree. As I mentioned in my piece, the practical history of the Reformed tradition around issues of race, including slavery, has painful examples that demonstrate the dangers of dismembering covenant into a means of protecting forms of white supremacy.

It is heartwarming to read Christina Wassell's points of common ground centering around practices of spirituality that can foster a spirit of communion between our two traditions. Catholic and Reformed theological dialogues reveal the difficulties of opening doors of relationship through doctrinal interchange, although significant breakthroughs have been made even on issues as central as baptism, which Wassell affirms and celebrates. But I see in Wassell's response further reason to share approaches to spiritual formation and practices as ways to push open doors of fellowship in our historically fractured relationship.

My parents named me with John Wesley in mind, not so much for his Methodism as for his evangelical spirit. But it was personally refreshing to see how Sarah Lancaster locates the five points of the Reformed tradition comfortably within the heritage of my namesake.

I continue to learn so much from Mark Ellingsen's careful and caring excavation of the Lutheran theological tradition, enriching the close commonalities I knew we shared. We'd still enjoy and be challenged by more dialogue around Luther's "two kingdoms" understanding. For most of my life, first for a time in politics and then in the church, I've been pushed toward "political theology," appreciating what a Reformed perspective can contribute—and also the voices of the Anabaptist tradition and others. Ellingsen's consistent plea for an ethic embracing the "joyful spontaneity" afforded by grace still may feel like a reach for many traditional Reformed folk. But I suspect that this has more to do with genetic temperament, and the effects of living in environments saturated with gray skies and rain, like the Netherlands and Scotland, than with any significant theological differences!

It's impossible to do justice to all that has been so graciously shared by these eleven partners. In closing I want to underscore important learnings. With several, including Robert Millet's fascinating theological journey, the essential communal qualities of Christian faith have been strongly affirmed in contrast to highly individualized expressions of following Jesus. (I know Ken Woodward but had never heard Millet's recounting of his biting quote about a personal tailor vs. a personal savior!) Yet, while not individualistic, following Jesus does have a personal dimension that goes far beyond the intellect. The Reformed tradition stands in continual need to develop and deepen its forms of spiritual practice that reach the soul as well as the mind.

There's a deep dialogue to be had around the nature of sin and the pathways of grace within the human personality. That's reflected in the responses of Ford, Wassell, Lancaster, and others to traditional Calvinist understandings of "total depravity." My own theological journey today moves down these pathways, encouraged by grandkids on my lap, but also by the resources of the Orthodox tradition, the wisdom of contemplatives like Thomas Merton and Richard Rohr, and much more.

It's fascinating that it is Pentecostal partner J. Terry Todd who reminds me, and all of us, of the relational, Trinitarian framework for our theology. I agree wholeheartedly. And for the Reformed tradition, I believe that at this point in history, our two most important dialogue partners are the Orthodox tradition and the Pentecostal tradition. In that vein, Todd encourages us to "bring on the whole cacophony of Christian voices, mirrored in the Acts experience of Pentecostal tongues." I say, absolutely.

VII. THE BAPTIST TRADITION
DAVID GUSHEE

One Account of a Baptist Way of Following Jesus

One summer Friday afternoon in 1978 a teenage boy named David Gushee wandered uninvited into a Southern Baptist church in Tysons Corner, Virginia. I had never attended worship at that church, but my then-girlfriend attended there with her family—though they were out of town. I was on my own, a total stranger to that congregation and whoever might have been in the building that day.

I walked into the church in something of a spiritual crisis. Two years before, I had left the Catholic Church of my mother and heritage but had not been able to shake, or to slake, an abiding spiritual hunger. The afternoon that I walked into that building, I was looking for something that I did not know how to name.

That Friday afternoon I accepted the invitation from the youth minister to a youth mini-golf and ice cream outing that evening. It was fun. There was another activity on Saturday night, which I also attended. The next day I came to that church on a Sunday morning for the first time. I returned for Sunday night service. That night, a youthful drama group from California offered sketches about Jesus and Christianity that to me were compelling.

I said yes to yet one more activity, a Monday night home Bible study. At that event, the teacher asked us to break into groups to discuss these questions:

What was your life like before you met Jesus?

How did you meet Jesus and commit your life to him?

How has your life changed?

What are you doing now to tell others about Jesus?

It was during this discussion that it became decisively clear to me that on the terms of this paradigm, I was not a Christian. I had not had a personal meeting with Jesus. There was no commitment, no before and after. My life had not changed. I had never told anyone about this Jesus that I did not know. This all came to me as shocking revelation.

I was hungry that night, asking questions, trying to sort it out—an obvious evangelistic prospect. One of the drama group leaders, still in town because their van (mysteriously) wouldn't start, asked if we could hang out after the Bible study. We drove around in my car, while I asked him all kinds of questions. By the end of that night, I was ready to "invite Jesus into my heart to become my Savior and Lord." I did that, in a rush of excitement, relief, and tears, and became a Christian on the terms that were presented to me that day.

THE BAPTIST TRADITION

Two weeks later I was baptized by full immersion. I immediately began the intensive round of personal and church activities that were expected in the version of the faith that the Southern Baptists of Providence Baptist Church were offering. That version "took," and I became a full-on born-again, Bible-reading, friend-evangelizing Baptist Christian. Within six months I felt sure I was called to become a Baptist pastor. My life had an entirely new direction.

That little congregation was hardly the idyllic haven of true Christianity that I thought it was at first appearance. They had their share of fissures and fractures, of divergent visions and fired ministers. But at that Ur-moment in my spiritual journey, they offered what I needed and was ready to hear. They taught me that being a "born-again," "Baptist" "Christian" "disciple of Jesus" meant something like this: aided by the Holy Spirit, to accept that Jesus had died on the cross to atone for my and the world's sins (i.e., "accepting Jesus Christ as my Savior") and to "commit my life to serving Jesus as Lord"—the one in charge of me.

Thus, the way of Jesus in this first primitive introduction involved both gift and task—the gift of a staggering sacrifice to atone and forgive me for my sins (I was aware that they were abundant), and the task of learning how to become a faithful servant of a new Lord, no longer my wretched self-curved-in-on-itself, but Jesus Christ. This latter project, it was soon clear, was demanding, open-ended, and lifelong—one never arrived, one was always on the way, there was always more to learn, more growing to do, more sin to repent for, more Bible to read and (better and better) understand, more people to (better and better) love, more millions to evangelize, and, of course, more Sunday School classes, church services, youth choirs, Bible studies, and mission seminars to attend.

I would not hesitate to put forward this basic paradigm of what it means to follow Jesus as foundational for me and far preferable to many available alternatives even today: Christianity as receiving the ultimate gift (of God's saving love in Christ) and undertaking the ultimate task (of reorienting one's life to serve Christ with everything). If one wants as close to a near-consensus Baptist vision of discipleship as might exist, I think that is it. I think it tracks with centuries of Baptist history, would be recognizable in most parts of the global Baptist world, and still deeply inspires the vision of many Baptist churches and Christians today.

By now, of course, in the year of our Lord 2022, many more complexities could be named, and much has changed in Baptist-land.

COMPLEXITIES: The good news, God's good gift, should not simply be reduced to Christ's atoning sacrifice for our sins. The mission of God in the world should be broadened to include a cosmic redemption that goes beyond individual souls, and therefore the mission of the church must go beyond discipleship training, personal evangelism, and world missions. The conversionist paradigm fits badly with a developmental-staged faith that often better reflects people's life experiences. Personal discipleship training needs to watch out for perfectionism and guilt-mongering. A social, ethical, political vision is needed and not just a personal one. Theology matters and not just a few Scripture nuggets and lots of personal-experiential religion. A historical sensibility is needed to compare and contrast Baptist ways with other ways and to understand the ebb and flow of Baptist patterns over time. Such awareness would lead, among other things, to seeing that the churches as covenanted communities of disciples, and not just earnestly striving individuals, is the longer Baptist heritage.

THE BAPTIST TRADITION

CHANGES: Southern Baptists in particular fractured not long after I entered the community. For one thing, a Calvinist vision surged. Such was entirely absent from my primal Baptist congregation, though admittedly a large part of Baptist history. Southern Baptist conservatives and fundamentalists (some, but not all of them, hardcore Calvinists) prevailed over moderates and liberals, and three denominations formed where once there had been one. Eventually, within an hour of walking into most any Baptist congregation in the U.S., you could tell where you were in Baptist life by social-ethical-political symbols and nudges from the platform or program. Southern Baptists in particular became part of the Religious Right from the 1980s onward and a huge part of what became #MAGATrumpvangelicalChristianity, which has little if any family resemblance to the serious Jesus-as-Savior-and-Lord Baptist Christianity that I cut my teeth on in 1978.

I find greater health and hope these days in global Baptist circles. I supervise PhD students from around the world and am an integral part of the educational efforts of the International Baptist Theological Study Centre in Amsterdam. I like conversations that are not dominated by the scorched-earth wounds and stuck arguments of 40 years of US religio-political warfare.

Imagine the young people today who are just as fired by spiritual hunger as that young man who walked into that church on a lovely afternoon in July 1978. Today they have so much more to navigate: Exactly which flavor of Baptist is this congregation? Do I vote the wrong way to be accepted here? Does this church offer a vision for following Jesus worth building a life on, and people who actually model it?

At the risk of hopeless anachronism, I yearn for Baptists to return to that long-ago message. God's love to human beings has been expressed in Jesus Christ. The best possible human life is to serve him as Lord.

Highlights of Responses from Other Christian Traditions

FOLLOWING JESUS INCLUDES BOTH GIFT AND TASK: After sharing his moving experience of "conversion" to the Christian faith, David Gushee, our Baptist CP, emphatically asserts that such a "conversion" is only the beginning of a lifelong journey.

Gushee elaborates by asserting what he claims is a "near-consensus Baptist vision of discipleship": Following Jesus involves BOTH "gift" AND "task"—accepting "the gift of a staggering sacrifice [by Jesus] to atone and forgive me for my sins" and committing to "the task of learning how to become a faithful servant of a new Lord [Jesus Christ]."

Gushee adds a claim that the task is broad: "The good news, God's good gift, should not simply be reduced to Christ's atoning sacrifice for our sins." Rather, "The mission of God in the world should be broadened to include a cosmic redemption that goes beyond individual souls." Gushee concludes that this broadening will require a "social, ethical, political vision," not just a "personal" vision." And living out this vision is BOTH an individual task AND a communal task.

Gushee rejects the idea that such a vision has been adequately captured by the significant number of Southern Baptists who "became part of the Religious Right from the 1980s onward and a huge part of what became #MAGATrumpvangelical-Christianity." If Gushee is right about that, this leaves open the question as to the contours of such a "social, ethical, political vision" that Christians should embrace.

What are the Contours of a Social, Ethical, and Political Vision?

There is strong affirmation from the other CPs of the need for Christians to embrace both the "gift" and the "task." But Michael King, drawing on his experience within his Anabaptist tradition, expresses concern that contemporary Christians may be gravely mistaken in believing that carrying out the "task" requires that Christians embrace non-Christian views regarding the meaning and exercise of "power." In his own words, whereas "earlier versions of Anabaptism offered "alternatives to the earthly principalities and powers," prophetically challenging "the often-unjust structures, institutions, ideologies, elemental spirits or socio-economic patterns of our day," at present "a growing number of us [Anabaptists] seem more interested in being aligned with the powers or even constructing ourselves into powers."

What, then, is an adequate set of Christian beliefs regarding a "social, ethical, political vision?" That is a question that, due to space limitations, was not adequately addressed by our CPs, but which begs for ongoing conversation. For your consideration, I embrace an ethical vision that starts with my enumeration of what I understand to be eight foundational Christian values.[1]

I then call for a strategy that I call "Freedom Within Bounds":

---

[1] These are positive relationships with God; physical life and health; caring relationships between persons; truth about all aspects of God's creation; justice, especially on behalf of the poor, marginalized, and oppressed among us; peace and reconciliation between persons and groups in conflict; flourishing of the natural environment; and fostering the human creation of beauty. Of course, no one Christian can focus on all these values. The biblical teaching about the nature of the body of Christ (see 1 Corinthians 12) is that each Christian should be fostering those Christian values that fit best with his/her gifts.

I have the freedom to choose means for fostering one or more of these Christian values, provided the means chosen are not destructive of these values.²

Questions for Future Conversations

Q1: Do you agree with the claim by David Gushee that following Jesus involves both the "gift" and "task" that he outlines? In not, what is the substance of your disagreement and what alternative position would you propose?

Q2: What do you believe are the contours of a "social, ethical, political vision" that Christians should seek to implement today in America?

Q3: What is your understanding of the nature of the "power" that Christians should be exercising as they seek to follow Jesus? How does your view fit, or not fit, with prevalent current views as to the meaning and exercise of "power" in contemporary American culture?

Q4: David Gushee points to a specific place and time where he had the conversion experience of being "born again." What does it mean to be "born again"? In light of what you believe this means, is it necessary to be able to point to a specific place and time for having such an experience? If not, what is a viable alternative position?

---

2 For an elaboration of the strategy I call "Freedom Within Bounds," see "My Ethical Project" (pp. 220-24) in my essay "Mathematics: Freedom Within Bounds" (pp. 206-230) in The Reality of Christian Learning: Strategies for Faith-Discipline Integration, edited by Harold Heie and David L. Wolfe. Grand Rapids, MI: Eerdmans, 1987.

Responding to Eleven Very Gracious Christian Friends

It was a treat reading the engagement of the entire *Following Jesus* team with my post laying out my understanding of Baptist ways of following Jesus.

I especially appreciated how my turn to spiritual autobiography elicited considerable storytelling from other sisters and brothers in Christ. There is something instructive there, I think. Certainly, many of our traditions make *testimony*, in one form or another, an important part of the discipleship journey. I cannot count the number of times I have been asked to "share my testimony," nor the occasions in which worship services included spontaneous or planned testimony times. While such testimony times *can* reinforce individualism and self-focus, at their best they serve as sources of instruction about the Christian journey. We teach each other about the spiritual journey with Christ through the stories we tell.

I would like to respond, however briefly, to each of the essays so graciously offered by our team. It was like a conversation with eleven very gracious Christian friends. We should do this more often!

To David Ford and the Orthodox tradition, with a nod also to Sarah Lancaster and the Wesleyan tradition, I want to heartily affirm the term "sanctification" with the meaning of real, actual, growth in holiness, to name what is supposed to happen in that never-ending journey of Christian discipleship. I have been struck by how few Baptist pastors and churches actually use the term. I also affirm the church as the community in which together, deploying all relevant resources of past and present, we pursue sanctification as both gift (of God's Spirit) and task (involving our effort). I see sanctification more as becoming fully human in Christ than as *theosis*, but that is an old argument, isn't it?

To Randall Balmer and the Anglicans, Sarah Lancaster, and Mark Ellingsen for the Lutherans, I want to reaffirm that 1) my conversionism remains strong, though I know it is not everyone's story, 2) the Wesleyan version that Sarah laid out really offers an enriching contrast with the Baptist paradigm I encountered, and 3) I cannot accept infant baptism as part of the conversionist paradigm, except perhaps as marking a kind of conversionist opportunity for many parents, as the depth of their Christian-formation responsibilities with their child is so powerfully symbolized.

I also want to put Terry Todd's poignant Pentecostal response together with Michael King's Anabaptist account and with Mark Ellingsen's post to affirm this truth: Baptist/evangelical conversionism *can* create spiritual morbidities when especially young or hyper-scrupulous people are unable to be convinced that their conversion is "sure" or has "taken." Add that to the constantly ramped-up fear of hell and this is a path to spiritual panic. The Lutheran perspective that we remain sinners who must repent again and again is a very helpful corrective here: Who among us is truly "converted"? And yet we semi-converted, semi-followers of Jesus are the ones on the journey of discipleship. Such paradoxes abound in the Christian life.

Wes Granberg-Michaelson (Reformed), Christina Wassell (Roman Catholic), Farris Blount (Black Baptist), and really most of the posts in one form or another worried about individualism and individualist tendencies in Baptist versions of Christianity, especially in our very individualist society. I agree. Such individualism can make Christians little more than church-hopping, church-shopping consumers, pulling us away (as Blount mentions) from thinking about where we can best serve to instead focus on where we can best *be served*. Individualism can also fragment churches theologically, as people have no framework of accepted authority to settle doctrinal differences. It can also make Christians and congregations utterly blind to their social, ethical, and political responsibilities.

I do agree with Todd, however, that the term "conscience," which can be collective but is sometimes quite lonely and individual, needs emphasis. I have indeed taken a number of conscientious stands in my career; they have been driven by my conscience and conviction, and they have sometimes broken with the convictions of the communities to which I belonged.

On the issue of what's my beef with the US Reformed types, Granberg-Michaelson's essay named it better than I ever have, and that kind of tactical/political Reformed theology bears no resemblance to what I see in winsome people like Granberg-Michaelson, and so many others—many of whom I have encountered in wintry climes in Michigan!

I would also like to take this opportunity to apologize to Wassell for my assumptions related to her parish and its relationship with Vatican II and the current pope. Thank you for your grace and for that clarification.

I want to thank Millet (LDS Church) for his storytelling related to the endless altar call from his own friend. That is truly bad form. Conversionism can be experienced as spiritually abusive. I am impressed that your friendship survived. That says much about your own Christian maturity and God's grace in and through you. Remind me to tell you about the time when I was 18 years old and I held open an altar call for 20 minutes in order to browbeat my ex-girlfriend into converting so that she could she be my "equally yoked" girlfriend once again. . . .

Finally, with special nods to Christopher Gehrz (Pietist) and Michael King (Anabaptist), and others as well, it is certainly true that my professional work has involved an awful lot of articulating Christian social ethics. (Thanks for several kind comments about my work!) I agree with Gehrz that being irenic is not enough, though it is a heckuva lot better than the irascibility so often encountered in Christian circles. Still, we need a social ethic. And developing that social ethic takes a lot of work—biblical, historical, theological, social-scientific, and every other kind of resource is needed to do it well. It also involves a willingness to take hard, definite stands and to make arguments against other views. It can be assumed to connect with and to create controversy. Some of what Christian ethics does challenges the world and its powers. All of it challenges the church.

There are indeed days where I wish for what seemed the relative simplicity of my new-convert days. My Christian vision was simpler. My sense of calling was simpler. Both church and world seemed simpler. But Christian life is a journey, and there is no going back, only forward.

I am glad to be on this journey with so many wonderful Christian kinfolk.

VIII. THE PIETIST TRADITION
CHRISTOPHER GEHRZ

A Week in the Life of a Pietist

In many ways, I represent the most unusual member of this gathering of Christian traditions. So, I hope you'll understand if my version of the lead essay seems atypical as well.

Please join me in imagining a week in the life of a Pietist seeking to follow Jesus.

THE POWER—AND LIMITS—OF CORPORATE WORSHIP

Let us first follow her to worship on Sunday morning. Immediately, we notice that "Pietist" is not found in the name of her church. If she worships with a congregation of the Evangelical Covenant Church, we might overhear some reference to those Christians' heritage as "missional Pietists." Something similar is possible, but still less likely, if we find ourselves in a Converge (Baptist), Evangelical Free, or formerly Augustana Lutheran church, since those are historical cousins of the Covenant, fellow offshoots of a mid-nineteenth-century revival in Sweden whose leading periodical was called *Pietisten*. Or if it's a Methodist, Moravian, or Brethren congregation that's particularly attentive to its history, we might happen to hear how John Wesley, Nikolaus von Zinzendorf, or Alexander Mack took inspiration from a now-defunct movement in early modern Europe called Pietism.

None of those instances is probable. For unlike every other participant in this year-long conversation, the Pietist Tradition has no ecclesial shape or institutional structure. And the number of Christians worldwide who identify as Pietist is vanishingly small.

Yet theologian Roger Olson claims that Pietism "became *the* main form of Protestantism" in North America (*The Story of Christian Theology*, p. 491). For if there is no Pietist movement, we might nonetheless discover what Olson calls "the Pietist ethos" in Lutheran, Wesleyan, Baptist, Anabaptist, Reformed, and other churches represented by other participants in this conversation.[3]

But if we're to recognize that ethos this Sunday morning, we first need to keep in mind what Pietist forefather Philipp Jakob Spener (1635-1705) wrote in the pivotal passage of the original movement's founding text, *Pia Desideria*: "It is by no means enough to have knowledge of the Christian faith, for

[3] Olson even claims overlap with Pentecostalism, his home tradition. Precisely because the Pietist ethos leavens so many different versions of Christianity, it would be a waste of scarce words to sketch all the differences. I've tried instead to emphasize what Pietists might have in common. To give some specificity, I've leaned most heavily on my own branch of Pietism, that stemming from the nineteenth-century renewal within Swedish Lutheranism that—after migration to the United States—gave rise to my home denomination (the Evangelical Covenant Church) and my employer of nearly 20 years (Bethel University).

Christianity consists rather of practice." So, while our Pietist might repeat the words of a creed or nod along with the theology presented from the pulpit, she has come to church this Sunday primarily to *experience* God through *practice*, not just to have her belief in God reaffirmed.

To put too fine a point on it: She is here to meet Jesus, not just to think about the idea of Christ. So even if she frets that she is participating in a version of Christianity prone to anti-intellectualism, she might admit that the most important part of the service is a simple hymn. Perhaps one by Lina Sandell, the greatest poet of the Swedish revival. Tears well up as our Pietist sings softly of a God who resembles both the heavenly father who gathers his children close to his chest and the mother hen who spreads gentle, holy wings around her chicks, a God who makes mercies known "day by day, and with each passing moment."

As that music fades and the preacher begins the sermon, our Pietist hopes not so much to hear an erudite exposition of Scripture as what Spener begged of his fellow Lutheran clergy: "plain but powerful" preaching that touches "the inner man or the new man"—or inner/new woman—"whose soul is faith and whose expressions are the fruits of life."

Of course, our Pietist may also encounter God through other means available in any Christian worship service: prayers, readings, and sacraments or ordinances. But in all these practices, she might find herself unable to shake the spiritual dissatisfaction that has always energized Pietism, for better and for worse. She might reproach herself for suspecting other Christians of going through the motions of rote repetition. Still, she worries that right belief too easily decays into a "dead orthodoxy" that makes no discernible difference in how believers live. Most of all, she longs for a Christianity more "authentic" than a religion of custom and culture.

She might then start to admit that Spener's critics weren't wrong to coin "Pietist" as a pejorative for Christians who seem to think themselves more pious than their neighbors. But our modern-day Pietist can't shake her desire for something more: the new life that starts with new birth; grace that doesn't just declare sinners just, but regenerates and sanctifies them.

The Devotional Life

And she has long since decided that Pietism's "living faith" depends on practices and experiences other than corporate worship led by a member of the clergy. So as Monday (or any other) morning dawns, we find our Pietist seeking God by herself, practicing the solitary piety of private devotions. She prays to a God who is always listening; she studies Scriptures inspired by a God who is always speaking.

In the pages of the Old and New Testaments, our Pietist seeks transformation, not information; relationship, not rules. For the Bible, as the Covenant Church has taught, is above all "an altar where we meet the living God." "Pietists love the Bible," explain Roger Olson and Christian Collins Winn, "not because it contains propositional truths about God to feed the mind, but because it is the principal medium for the Christian's relationship with God" (*Reclaiming Pietism*, p. 99). In God's written word, our Pietist meets the living Word and walks alongside him—traveling her own version of the Emmaus Road until Jesus' teaching leaves her heart burning within her.

But just as Cleopas did not walk alone, our Pietist knows that her relationship with God through Christ must intersect with her relationship with other followers of Jesus. The next evening, she repeats the same spiritual disciplines, but now in the company of a few others. By meeting weekly with her small group, she repeats the oldest, most influential innovation of the original Pietist movement. Even before Spener published *Pia Desideria*, a lawyer named Johann Jakob Schütz convinced him to convene *collegia pietatis* outside of their larger congregation—little churches within the larger church (*ecclesiolae in ecclesia*) whose members worked through prayer and study toward a closer connection with God and each other.

While that idea went back at least as far as the early years of Martin Luther's reformation (or the late medieval Brethren of the Common Life), it was the German Pietist movement that established small group Bible study as a staple of modern Christianity. Like much of the Pietist ethos, that kind of collective practice has become so pervasive as to seem mundane. Yet "inoffensive as [Spener's conventicles] might sound," explains historian Alec Ryrie, "they marked a decisive shift in religious power" (*Protestants*, p. 162)—from the clergy to the laity, from the church hierarchy to the common priesthood. When my Swedish ancestors, like their Haugean counterparts in Norway, met in their small groups, they were breaking laws established in protection of state churches that jealously guarded those institutions' right to control the meaning of God's word. The very existence of the small group underscores that, for Pietists, no single person and no single understanding of Scripture has the authority of the Bible itself, the interpretation of which requires multiple perspectives, lest old error maintain itself against the correction of new insights.

Of course, that doesn't happen if the small group simply 6453. But if our Pietist's version of the *collegia* is anything like Spener's original, it spans the theological and political divisions of its time. It serves as an enduring witness to the original Pietist desire that Christians cease their "angry polemics" and "needless controversy" and restore something of the unity that Jesus prayed for and Paul exhorted.

Making Faith Active in Love

At the same time, such devotional practices also highlight a danger inherent to the Pietist Tradition. Mennonite scholar Robert Friedmann, for example, scorned Pietism as "a quiet conventicle-Christianity which is primarily concerned with the inner experience of salvation and only secondarily with the expression of love toward the brotherhood, and not at all in a radical world transformation" (*Mennonite Piety Through the Centuries*, p. 11). As she heads into the second half of her week, our Pietist might worry that she's being "too heavenly minded to be any earthly good."

But after she wakes up the next morning and continues her regular daily routines at work, home, and elsewhere, she may be conscious of the other great legacy of German Pietism: August Hermann Francke's commitment to make faith active in love of others.

For Francke (1663-1727), personal conversion to Jesus Christ sparked social action: the creation of an orphanage and schools that took in poor children; a university that trained pastors, missionaries, and military chaplains; a pharmacy that healed illnesses; and a publishing house that churned out affordable Bibles and devotional literature. But even if our Pietist doesn't work in education, health care, or what we'd tend to think of as Christian ministry, Francke would tell her that Christian faith can be made lovingly active in a myriad of ways. Whatever her vocation and wherever her setting, advised Francke, the Pietist should carry out her "calling joyfully and cheerfully to the glory of God and [her] neighbor's good without greed."

As the week continues and these God-glorifying, neighbor-loving practices repeat, our Pietist lives out her new life in Christ as the Covenant theologian Don Frisk defined it, following Jesus by following him into the world:

Whatever form conversion takes it will be characterized by entrance into *freedom*—the freedom which comes through the presence of Christ in one's life—and by involvement in Christ's mission to the world. To be converted to Christ is always in a sense to be converted (turned) to the world. It is to see the world through the eyes of Christ, to share his compassion, to perceive his will for the world, and to strive to follow it.

Highlights of Responses from Other Christian Traditions

AGREEING ON THREE ELEMENTS FOR CHRISTIAN LIVING: While acknowledging that "The Pietist tradition has no ecclesial shape or institutional structure [unlike the other Christian traditions participating in our ecumenical conversation]," Chris Gehrz, our Pietist CP, proposes three foci for Christian living that constitute a "Pietist ethos" that is also embraced by many of these other traditions.

The first focus is on "Meeting Jesus in Worship Services." Gehrz asserts that "The typical pietist Christian comes to church to 'meet Jesus, not just to think about the idea of Jesus'" (acknowledging that this focus makes some pietists "prone to anti-intellectualism").

The second focus is on "The Devotional Life." Gehrz observes that "As Monday (or any other morning) dawns, we find our Pietist seeking God by herself, practicing the solitary piety of private devotions," adding that "In the pages of the Old and New Testaments, our Pietist seeks transformation, not information; relationship, not rules." This second focus is often implemented in "small groups" since "For the Pietist, no single person or no single understanding of Scripture has the authority of the Bible itself, whose interpretation requires multiple perspectives, lest old error maintain itself against the correction of new insights."

The third focus of the "pietist Ethos" is on "Loving my Neighbor and Contributing to God's Redemption of the World." Gehrz asserts that "As the week continues [after the Sunday worship service], . . . our Pietist lives out her new life in Christ, following Jesus by following him into the world." Gehrz favorably quotes Pietist theologian Don Frisk: "Whatever form conversion takes, it will be characterized by involvement in Christ's mission to the world. To be converted to Christ is always in a sense to be converted (turned) to the world. It is always to see the world through the eyes of Christ, to share his compassion, to perceive his will for the world, and to strive to follow it."

A chorus of responses from the other CPs reveal strong agreement with the three foci enumerated by Gehrz. But a number of our other CPs question the extent to which the Pietist tradition actually practices the third focus. Five examples are worthy of consideration.

Michael King, our Anabaptist CP, notes the observation made by some Mennonite preachers that "Pietistic hymns can generate a me-and-God as opposed to us-and-God or God-and-the world Christianity."

Randall Balmer, our Anglican CP, observes that "religious fervor, the kind of spirituality favored by Pietists, is difficult to sustain over a long period of time." This is because "A highly rational theology" provides "regularity and predictability, whereas an emphasis on a warm-hearted piety can lead in all sorts of unpredictable directions."

Possibly the most telling concern was expressed by David Gushee, our Baptist CP and a world-renowned Christian ethicist. Gushee argues that a "devout person" should be exemplified not only by "church going and praying," but also by exemplifying "high standards of morality." And Gushee wonders whether this added dimension is adequately emphasized in the Pietist tradition.

Farris Blount, our Black Church CP, presents a pointed example of Gushee's concern when he wonders whether the "engagement in the world" envisioned by Pietists is expansive enough to include "collective action to create systemic change," especially the systemic change needed to "address the economic, social and political gaps that exist in our society."

ELABORATING ON "HIGH STANDARDS FOR CHRISTIAN MORALITY": By now the reader should have discerned, in much of what you have read in this book up to this point, the pressing need to avoid a false choice. Whatever ways in which your Christian tradition gives expression to the importance of providing resources for spiritual growth, including worship services and emphasis on a rich devotional life, that is not a sufficient vision for daily Christian living. In addition to that important emphasis, Christians in every Christian tradition need to receive instruction and be presented with means to live out "high standards for Christian morality." It is both/and, not either/or. And a good place to start with such instruction would be to read David Gushee's book *Introducing Christian Ethics: Core Convictions for Christians Today.*

Questions for Future Conversations

Q1: To what extent do you embrace the three foci of the "Pietist Ethos" proposed by Chris Gehrz? If you have reservations, what are they?

Q2: To what extent does your tradition encourage its members to give expression to the three foci proposed by Gehrz? If you perceive a weakness in strategies for implementing one or more of these three areas, what would you propose for strengthening them?

Q3: Farris Blount wonders whether adherents to the Pietist tradition (or any other Christian tradition) pay sufficient attention to creating "systemic change" in societal structures—change needed to address the root causes, not just the symptoms, of existing economic, social, and political gaps in our society. Do you agree with Blount? If so, what steps do you think need to be taken to address his concern? If you disagree with Blount, why?

Is Pietism Really a Tradition? Is It Evangelicalism? And What of Justice?

Above all else, count me relieved that my unusual approach to the lead essay format seems to have connected with so many of my conversation partners. Knowing that the typical response to the word "Pietism" in the twenty-first century is either non-recognition ("What's that?") or mis-recognition ("Oh, you mean legalism"—or "anti-intellectualism" or "quietism"), I hoped for nothing more than trying to help people see Pietism from the inside-out.

If no one else here would come to the end of my essay and call themselves a Pietist—though I'm happy to find a Pentecostal cousin!—I do think it's telling just how many people in this conversation heard something of their own experience of following Jesus in my imagined narrative of one Pietist's week. Perhaps it offers some small confirmation of Roger Olson's thesis about the pervasiveness of the Pietist ethos. Given how rarely music has come up over the past months, I'm especially delighted that everyone from Mennonites to Methodists to Mormons resonated with my paragraph about singing the hymns of Lina Sandell.

But by the same token, I can understand why Granberg-Michaelson came to the end of my essay and still found it hard "to understand Pietism (with a capital 'P') as a distinct Christian tradition." Wassell was spot on in describing Pietism as "a strain of religious expression that hasn't demanded a denomination, per se, and the trappings that come with it. Rather, this tradition seems content to be an influence that flows through many of the Protestant strains represented in our conversation."

Perhaps Pietists never really had the option to demand denominational trappings. As Balmer perceptively observed, Pietism "provided a means to circumvent calcified and unresponsive institutions. All well and good. But a kind of sociological inevitability kicks in at some point, and as the faith becomes routinized and institutionalized, a new wave of scholasticism takes root—and thereby sets the stage for a new Pietistic revival of some sort." In that sense, an institutionalized Pietism is impossible.

(Here I thought of Ellingsen, who understandably circled back to many of our earlier points of agreement and disagreement in pondering a reunion of the Pietist child with its Lutheran mother. In my response to his essay, I had quoted his fellow Haugean Pietist Lutheran Gracia Grindal—a translator of Lina Sandell, among her many other accomplishments. Lamenting the decline of Pietism within this country's largest Lutheran denomination, Grindal acknowledged that "a personal and individual experience simply cannot be passed on to the next generation through doctrine or structure. It tends to go cold." And yet she hoped that what she took to be the spiritual coldness of contemporary Lutheranism might spark a new Pietist renewal. And so the cycle goes. . . .)

When he invited me to participate, I wasn't sure why Heie would give one of twelve precious spaces in this conversation to something that is more a common ethos than a body of Christians sharing a sense of identity. So why include Pietists in the mix?

I suspect that Wassell may have put her finger on it, in concluding that my hypothetical Pietist sounded like "a thoughtful, if a bit overly self-conscious, Evangelical." Who in this conversation, after all, speaks for the wing of Protestantism that still claims an enormous segment of the American Christian population? Ultimately, I think that role will fall to Todd more than anyone, since Pentecostalism accounts for a growing share of Evangelicals worldwide. But there's enough affinity between Pietism and Evangelicalism that I can also understand why Granberg-Michaelson was left wondering "what characterizes Pietism from American Evangelicalism."

For much of their shared history, the answer would be: not much. It's undeniable that Pietism helped to inspire the evangelical awakenings of the eighteenth century (see W. R. Ward, who starts his "global intellectual history" of Evangelicalism with Philipp Spener) and the nineteenth century; Roger Olson even subdivides Evangelicalism into "Pietist-Pentecostal" and "Puritan-Reformed" paradigms. It's only in the twentieth century that we see space widen between the two, enough that my home denomination would refuse to join the National Association of Evangelicals. As historian Kurt Peterson has argued, leaders and scholars in the Evangelical Covenant Church identified themselves with what we're calling the Pietist Tradition because they wanted to chart a "third way" between the liberal theology of mainline Protestantism and what they suspected to be the lingering fundamentalism of Billy Graham's neo-evangelical movement.

So what distinguishes Pietists from Evangelicals? There's still significant overlap—in myself, among others—but I think Gushee's response to my essay can help us start to recognize the differences. He didn't call them Evangelicals, but I suspect that many of those Protestants number among the "coldhearted, coldblooded, doctrinaire, politicized, and sometimes amoral Christian folks" whom Gushee finds so "befuddling." For Pietists, what's still most important is what Gushee called the "vital, living relationship with Jesus Christ" and "[demonstrating] this vital, loving heartbeat of faith in our daily interactions with others," not the traits that tend increasingly to define contemporary evangelicalism: "affirming orthodoxy, voting for the right party, and owning the libs."

First, "affirming orthodoxy." This far removed from the Modernist-Fundamentalist split of the early twentieth century, Evangelicals don't like to be identified with the latter term, but they still love to define themselves as guarding "historic orthodoxy" against the former threat. And they don't necessarily mean the centuries-old doctrines that Ford and Ellingsen emphasized in their responses to my essay (though I appreciate Ford's encouragement to consider more carefully the relationship between propositions and piety), but beliefs about issues that may strike other Christians as being of secondary or tertiary importance, such as the nature of human origins or gender roles, or a particular way of understanding the inspiration, authority, and truthfulness of Scripture.

Such theological gatekeeping aggravates the divisions within Christianity that Pietists have always abhorred and sought to transcend. Moreover, it makes possible Gushee's combination of the adjectives "doctrinaire" and "coldhearted." (Tellingly, the Covenant Church has said in recent years that it is "evangelical, but not exclusive" and "biblical, but not doctrinaire.") The fear of "dead orthodoxy" that keeps inspiring irruptions of Pietism is no longer about the Nicene Creed or the Augsburg Confession; Pietists instead see it among some Evangelical defenders of the Chicago Statement on Biblical Inerrancy or the Danvers Statement about "biblical manhood and womanhood." Not only because they seem to us to be "majoring in the minors," but because Pietists ask what difference this kind of faith makes in one's life—whether it inspires love of others, or something more toxic. What else but "dead orthodoxy" do we call it when some Evangelicals insist that the Bible inerrantly defines rigidly distinct gender roles yet manifest that belief in misogyny and abuse?

Second, "voting for the right party, and owning the libs." At this point in US history, the term "Evangelical" is so closely bound up with partisan politics that many Evangelicals themselves are ready to drop the term. But if I'm right that a Pietist "longs for a Christianity more 'authentic' than a religion of custom and culture," then no Pietist has much at stake in a "culture war" fought on behalf of ostensibly "traditional" values.

Which is why I acknowledged in my lead essay that some Pietists have embraced quietism. (Understandably, like Todd, I find myself yearning for more "quietude, soundlessness, even the apophatic[.]") But for those of us who want to be "heavenly-minded" and yet seek "earthly good," the most common Pietist strategy has not been political activism. Instead, most of us imitate what the Brethren scholar Dale Brown called

"Christ the servant of culture." By contrast to the five models of Christ sketched by Richard Niebuhr[4]—in particular, the one that leads Christians to seek to control their culture—Brown suggested that Pietists "neither . . . try to get on the top in order to make things come out the way we think they should or refuse to become involved at all." Instead, we seek at once to "[love] the world for which Christ died," by making faith active in loving service, even as our commitment to conversional piety helps us not conform to the world's more destructive patterns.

(As someone who straddled the Anabaptist and Pietist traditions, Dale Brown would surely appreciate King's comment: "[T]he tenderness that watches o'er the troubled ones of us safely in God's bosom gathering can be a key source of returning to the world healed enough to care for it.")

I think that explains as well as anything why Pietists would be as likely to support evangelical ministries of compassion and mercy like those of Samaritan's Purse as they are to reject the staunchly right-wing politics of that organization's leader, Franklin Graham. But it leaves open the question raised by several responses and posed most clearly by Blount:

---

4 By the way, Richard and Reinhard Niebuhr grew up within yet another of the small American denominations influenced by Pietism: the Evangelical Synod of North America. I knew it would be foolish to try to name all such bodies in my own short essay, so thanks to Ellingsen for mentioning another in his response: the Church of the Lutheran Brethren. I could also add the handful of historically Norwegian "free Lutherans" who resisted absorption into what became the ELCA, plus the historically Finnish congregations of the Apostolic Lutheran movement, which descend from another member of the nineteenth-century Pietist revival movement in Scandinavia: Lars Levi Laestadius. I'll leave it for Lancaster to decide whether to discuss the United Brethren (now part of the United Methodist Church but originally the foremost result of the Pietistic revival led by Martin Boehm and Philip William Otterbein) or the Brethren in Christ (who describe themselves as having Wesleyan as well as Pietist and Anabaptist origins).

FOLLOWING JESUS

. . . [H]ow does the Pietist suggest we deal with and pursue collective action to create systemic change? I can clearly see that Pietists support collective action to solve social ills—how else would [August Hermann] Francke have been able to create schools, an orphanage, and a publishing house to aid his community if not for the help of others? But each of these efforts appears to try and address the symptom of the ill and not the cause. An orphanage can take care of children who are poor, but it does not necessarily alter the societal conditions that create poor children and the need for orphanages in the first place. A publishing house can provide affordable resources, but it does not appear to decrease the ever-increasing cost of goods that widen the gulf between the wealthy and everyone else.

It's a clear weakness of my own tradition, one I named last month in my own response to Gushee. And it's why—whether or not Pietism deserves to be a part of this project—I'm happy to participate in this conversation. No tradition here follows Jesus perfectly, and I'm glad now to recede from prominence and go back to what I enjoy most about *Following Jesus*: the chance it gives me to listen to and learn from others.

IX. The Wesleyan Tradition
Sarah Lancaster

Holiness of Heart and Life

Other participants in this project have told their stories about how they came to participate in the tradition they represent in these conversations. My own story is quite straightforward. My father was a Methodist preacher, and my mother had been a Methodist missionary in India before she married my father. I was baptized as an infant in the Methodist Church (before a merger made it the United Methodist Church), so I have been in this tradition my entire life.

Of course, this tradition contains the same varieties of thought (conservative or progressive, evangelical or liberal) that are found in many other traditions. There have been divisions over various matters, such as race and slavery, lay rights, women's ordination, etc. (and we face division now over LGBTQ++ issues), but none of these "various views" are distinctive to Wesleyans. British and American Methodism have taken slightly different form in their different contexts, and as "foreign" mission activity was carried out separately by both British and North American Methodists, those differences were to some extent transported globally. All of us acknowledge our start in John Wesley's evangelical revival, so I will start with the history we hold in common before noting further various views.

When John and Charles Wesley led the Methodist movement during the eighteenth-century English Evangelical Revival, they were operating as priests within the Church of England. They did not intend to form a church, but rather they followed the model of organizing religious societies to call people already in church to follow Jesus more faithfully. For Wesley, Methodists were people who pursued "holiness of heart and life, inward and outward conformity in all things to the revealed will of God," imitating Jesus "more particularly in justice, mercy, and truth, or universal love filling the heart and governing the life" (*Advice to the People Called Methodists*). Wesley believed God raised up Methodists "[t]o reform the nation and, in particular, the Church; to spread scriptural holiness over the land" ("Large Minutes" of the Methodist Conference). In this brief account of what it means to follow Jesus in the Wesleyan tradition, I will explore the idea of scriptural holiness at the heart of the Wesleyan tradition.

EXCURSUS: *In my younger years, few in my orbit knew much about John Wesley's life and less about his theology. Wesley saw his primary task as conveying important theological ideas to ordinary people rather than to scholars. Because he produced no systematic theology, but rather did his theological reflection in sermon form to address specific practical matters, he was not often regarded even by those in his tradition as a theologian of consequence. Since the middle of the twentieth* century, there has been an effort to recognize his theological work and share it more broadly with people for their daily living. We are in a time of recovery and education. As a result, consciousness of the ideas I express in this essay may not yet be high among congregants; for instance, few people I know would ordinarily use the words "holiness" or "perfection," but as I teach Wesleyan ideas in various settings, the general reaction by people who have never heard them before is, "Oh, now I understand why I am Methodist." So, I think people have been formed in certain ways of thinking, even if not explicitly taught.

John Wesley's understanding of holiness can only be understood against the background of his understanding of human nature. For Wesley, Adam was created in the moral image of God, with love filling his soul and directing his actions. Adam had full liberty to remain in this state or to lose it. While he remained in the state God intended, he was happy. Adam's state changed, though, and with the fall, the nature God had given to Adam was marred, opening him to be ruled by other affections besides love (for instance, fear and anger), and crippling the love he was made for. The "one thing needful" for human beings is for Christ to renew our fallen nature, to restore us to wholeness so that we may again love God above all else and love everything else as God loves it. This renewal in holiness brings with it the happiness for which we were made.

This restoration happens as we follow Jesus. Wesley speaks of "salvation" in such a way that it includes not only what happens after death but also what happens in this life. If there is any "doctrinally distinct" center to Methodism, it is the way of salvation. Wesley's nuanced understanding of salvation includes serious attention to both justification and sanctification. Everything he describes in the "way of salvation" is initiated and empowered by grace (understood as the power and presence of God). In justification we truly and deeply learn through Jesus Christ that God loves us as dear children, we know we are forgiven, and we receive Christ's imputed righteousness. Because new birth (used alongside the image of adoption, this metaphor stresses a real change in us and not just a change in status) accompanies justification, we may begin to model our lives after the one we follow, learning from Jesus how to love properly. Sanctification consists of growing in holiness—understood as perfect love, namely "love excluding sin; love filling the heart, taking up the whole capacity of the soul" ("The Scripture Way of Salvation" §I.9). As we follow Jesus and imitate Jesus' love, we learn again to love as God loves, thereby becoming more who God created us to be. We are really changed by following Jesus.

Even though Methodists worked for individual hearts to be changed, Wesley understood Christianity to be "social" (not solitary) religion, and therefore even growth in holiness is "social." Being a child of God (justified) meant living as a child of God (sanctified). The movement was organized in small groups for members to talk openly with each other about the state of their souls, to encourage and, if necessary, admonish one another to follow Jesus more faithfully. We grow in God's love as we open ourselves to one another. Following Jesus to grow in holiness, then, was not finally individualistic and private, but rather took place in community.

Methodist societies were governed by three General Rules: Do no harm, do good, and attend upon the ordinances of God (in public worship and private devotion). These three rules guide us in expressing holy love. They direct attention to loving relationship with God and to those around us, and to the consequences of our behavior for society. Later generations have adopted the language of "social holiness" to refer to the way we show love of neighbor, especially the poor and the vulnerable. Even in the eighteenth century, Wesley had incipient understanding that systems and structures could do harm. He opposed the practice of slavery, and he connected the production of spirituous liquor to the grain shortage that deprived the poor of bread.

Over time, as the movement within a church has become itself ecclesial, this pattern of mutual confession in small groups has diminished, although there are sometimes attempts to revive them. Even so, there can be communal confession on a large scale. The "Wesleyan" tradition includes churches that began by breaking off from the original Methodist Episcopal Church because of racism (African Methodist Episcopal Church, African Methodist Episcopal Church Zion, and later from the MEC South the Christian Methodist Episcopal Church). In 2000, following our tradition of repentance in community, The United Methodist Church General Conference (a representative legislative body) held a liturgical Act of Repentance to acknowledge the racism of the past and commit to healing division between our churches. In 2004, The United Methodist Church held a similar service to repent for racism against those African Americans who remained in this church and to commit to a more inclusive future. In 2012, The United Methodist General Conference held another service to repent of harm done by the church to indigenous people in North America. Because the Acts took place in a representative body, members in local congregations may not have been entirely aware and involved, so the impact has not been as widespread as one would hope. Nevertheless, I value the way our heritage can be a resource to remind us that seeking holiness involves accountability before God.

Some of Wesley's complex theology has been stressed differently in different churches. I think it would be commonly held that holiness is love, but expressing love may take different forms. Some will seek holiness through countercultural behaviors, others will recognize it in struggle against oppression, others look for a powerful internal experience of God. This means that people in the same tradition may commit themselves to following Jesus somewhat differently—for instance in abstaining from alcohol, in protesting injustice, in seeking emotional experiences of God in prayer and worship.

John Wesley was so confident in God's ability to heal us that he taught a doctrine of "perfection" or entire sanctification (perfect love in this life). He acknowledged that perfection might happen gradually or instantaneously, but he urged people to expect it in this life. Expecting to be made more loving opens us to God's work to make us more loving. John's brother Charles was less sure we could receive perfect love before the point of death. John did not insist that everyone must or would be entirely sanctified before death, but he did encourage everyone to expect it. Expectation of perfect love should lead us to follow Jesus more closely as we seek this gift. The tradition that has followed him has had various ways of thinking about perfection: sometimes to ignore or dismiss it (no one can be perfect, not even in love), and at other times insisting upon it (in an instantaneous cleansing).

All these expressions of holiness may exist in a single church, but they may also characterize different churches in the tradition. For instance, there are "holiness" churches that stress entire sanctification and encourage lifestyles that avoid common cultural behaviors that are either considered sinful or could lead to sin (for instance smoking, drinking, some forms of dancing), while predominantly African American churches stress justice and liberation, and more evangelical churches call people to conversion experiences.

THE WESLEYAN TRADITION

In the Wesleyan tradition, following Jesus means being a child of God and living appropriately in that relationship. However differently holiness may be conceived, it is a common conviction that God empowers us to live in the power of the Holy Spirit so that we may work with God in God's intention to restore the world to what God created us to be.

Highlights of Responses from Other Traditions

WEDDING BOTH JUSTIFICATION AND SANCTIFICATION: Sarah Lancaster, our Wesleyan CP, joins the chorus of other CPs who reject a false choice by embracing BOTH a focus on one's personal relationship with Jesus AND a focus on living out the teachings of Jesus in daily life.

Lancaster asserts that this "wedding" was at the heart of John Wesley's vision for Methodism: "For Wesley, Methodists were people who pursued 'holiness of heart and life, inward and outward conformity in all things to the will of God' imitating Jesus 'more particularly in justice, mercy, and truth, or universal love filling the heart and governing the life.'"

In theological terms, Lancaster is pointing to the wedding of "justification" and "sanctification": "In justification we truly and deeply learn through Jesus Christ that God loves us as dear children, we know we are forgiven, and we receive Christ's imputed righteousness. Because new birth . . . accompanies justification, we may begin to model our lives after the one we follow, learning from Jesus how to love properly. Sanctification consists of growing in holiness."

Elaborating further, Lancaster reports that "Even though Methodists worked for individual hearts to be changed, Wesley understood Christianity to be 'social' (not solitary) religion and therefore even growth in holiness is 'social,'" and "Wesley had incipient understanding that systems and structures [of society] could do harm."

Lancaster further adds an observation that Methodists express their commitment to Wesley's vision in different ways. For example, "There are 'holiness churches that . . . encourage lifestyles that avoid common cultural behaviors that are considered sinful or could lead to sin (for instance smoking, drinking . . .), while predominantly African American churches stress justice and liberation, and more evangelical churches call people to conversion experiences."

A number of the other CPs applaud the Wesleyan wholistic approach to Christian living ("holiness of both heart and life"). But a few CPs express some concerns.

A first concern, which Lancaster acknowledges, is that while Wesley's vision may appear to be a basis for unity, in practice there have been deep divisions within Methodism about such issues as slavery, layperson rights, and women's ordination; and, now, over LGBTQ++ issues.

A second concern, expressed by Farris Blount, our Black Church CP, calls into question the idea that different Methodist congregations can choose to express their Christian commitment in "different ways." Blount asserts that "there are certain tenets of the Christian faith that are required and not optional," citing his belief that "To follow Jesus . . . means being concerned with the plight of those who are experiencing oppression or inequality. . . . So, being concerned with justice in the world is not an option for a follower of Jesus but a requirement."

In her end-of-the-month posting, Lancaster responds to Farris, saying that she "certainly did not intend to imply that social justice was optional. . . . Rather, what she wanted to indicate is that some will stress social action more than others."

I believe it is accurate to suggest that John Wesley was a "reforming fire" in his time. This raises the question as to who will be the "reforming fires" in our day, a question about which I will now share my personal reflections.

THE NEED FOR DISSIDENTS AS "REFORMING FIRES" I believe that all Christian traditions need to be alert to the possibility of their traditions transitioning from heartfelt renewal movements to lifeless moribund traditions that have succumbed to the allures of the cultures in which they are embedded.

Therefore, I believe that the present leaders and their followers within any Christian tradition need to listen carefully to those dissidents within their traditions who believe that the tradition has been compromised by non-Christian beliefs prevalent in the surrounding culture, on the basis of which they are passionately pleading for reform. Don't write off such dissidents as troublemakers. Don't silence them! They may be the "reforming fires" that are presently needed.

As all readers of this book and some of my previous publications and my website will know, I believe that the place to start such careful listening is to "provide a safe and welcoming space" for dissidents to express their disagreements with some tenets that currently pervade their traditions, to be followed by respectful and loving conversations about these disagreements.

Questions for Future Conversations

Q1: What is your assessment of the wholistic vision for Christian beliefs and living that John Wesley envisioned for Methodism? If you have disagreements, what are they? And, what alternative positions would you take?

Q2: Do you share Farris Blount's belief that "being concerned with justice in this world is not an option for a follower of Jesus, but a requirement"? If not, why not?

Q3: Sarah Lancaster reports that "John Wesley was so confident in God's ability to heal us that he taught a doctrine of 'perfection' or entire sanctification (perfect love in this life)," although she acknowledges that "the language of perfection is rarely used in [Methodist] congregations." What is your assessment of this belief held by John Wesley?

Q4: Sarah Lancaster reports that Christians within the Wesleyan tradition believe that Christians are called to **"work with God** in God's intention to restore the world to what God created us to be" (emphasis mine). What do you think it means to "partner with God" toward the realization of God's redemptive purposes?

Q5: John Wesley organized the Methodist movement around "small groups" where, in community, participants can talk to each other about the status of their Christian pilgrimages. What is your assessment of this strategy? Have you participated in such small group conversations among Christians? If so, how well did they go?

Deepening Community in Conversation

I am grateful for the ways that other partners in this conversation (especially Balmer, Todd, and Ford) have shared what they know about the tradition I represent. This conversation is valuable in many ways, not the least of which is to show that we actually do pay attention to each other as we follow Jesus. The realization that others have paid attention to my tradition

THE WESLEYAN TRADITION

deepens the sense of community I feel with other Christians.

I will give some short responses to items that were specifically named. King was interested in the imminent division over LGBTQ++ issues, and Todd also named this problem. It has been announced that the Global Methodist Church will launch on May 1, 2022, although many practical details will take time, and the new church will function "transitionally" for many months. The new GMC will share with the UMC much doctrinal material. King's observation that this division involves holiness, perfection, and social creeds is correct. Sadly, I have little wisdom to share at this painful point other than I think both GMC and UMC are trying to be faithful in following Jesus, but many people have profound differences of thinking about how that faithfulness should be expressed. It remains to be seen whether and how we may be able to work together in matters where our faithful following might be closer. There also may continue to be differences that have to be worked out among those who remain in the UMC.

Blount wondered about the place of social justice in my essay—is it simply a choice among other options or is it a requirement for a follower in the Wesleyan tradition? I certainly did not intend to imply that social justice was optional; the theology we have received calls all of us to act on behalf of those who suffer. I also believe the commitment to social justice is widely held. Rather, what I wanted to indicate is that some will stress social action more than others. I have been present when some folks in the tradition feel the need to call other folks to greater action when other things, such as personal conversion and personal behavior, have become the main focus.

Wassell found many commonalities between our traditions but wondered how we pursue holiness non-liturgically. In the

United Methodist Church, we do not have a fixed, formal liturgy, so there can be variety in worship. However, we do follow the liturgical year and we acknowledge the real presence of Christ in the Eucharist, even though we do not attempt to explain how this presence is possible.

Millet asked about the distinction between imputed righteousness and implanted righteousness. Wesley speaks of both because he finds a place for both justification and sanctification in the way of salvation. In justification, we are pardoned not because of anything we have done for ourselves but because of what Jesus Christ has done for us. Christ's righteousness is imputed to us. But with justification, sanctification also begins. We are empowered to live a holy life so God "implants" or "imparts" righteousness as we grow in love. So, imputed righteousness is the ground of our acceptance with God, but then the fruit of that acceptance is that we are actually changed as we reflect God's love more and more.

So, finally we arrive at sanctification and the possibility of perfection, about which a few expressed nervousness. Wesley himself had to continually explain his ideas in the face of great criticism. I will try to highlight and explain some ideas that may not eliminate nervousness, but I hope will improve understanding.

Let me say first that the language of perfection is rarely used in congregations that I know. During the pandemic when it was hard to worship in person, my husband and I took the opportunity to worship in many different United Methodist congregations across the country (we visited in 40 states and the UK). I can say from this experience that I heard many sermons about love, but only one actually referenced the Wesleyan doctrine of perfection. For most congregants, the kinds of questions that my conversation partners want to know more about are not very pressing because the language of perfection is not regularly used to express the call to learn from Jesus how to love. Still, I will answer as best I can about the things that have been wondered. I must also say that my perspective has been formed specifically within the United Methodist Church, and I cannot speak for the situations and experiences of all Wesleyans (for instance, Nazarenes).

First, let me address whether we can be made perfect (entirely sanctified) in this life. Because the Wesley brothers themselves had some differences regarding this point, I do not think the timing for arriving at the goal is the essential matter. The essential thing to realize about this doctrine is that relationship with God can really make us more loving, and yes, that happens in this life. And as I noted in my main post, expectation draws us forward.

It is also important to give some account of what our role is in this process. John Wesley does use the word "strive" when he talks about perfection. This word refers to the way we work to respond to God's work in our lives. John Wesley's way of putting this point was "First, God works; therefore you *can* work. Secondly, God works; therefore you *must* work." In other words, God makes it possible for us to follow Jesus in love, and we must do so in order to grow. We work with God, but we do not finally "achieve" perfection (entire sanctification) through our work. If sin is removed, it is an act of God, not an accomplishment by us. The way we navigated this matter in the full communion agreement with the Evangelical Lutheran Church in America was to say "the UMC sets no limit to God the Holy Spirit's activity and power in this present life" (*Confessing Our Faith Together*, para. 27). Unless and until God acts to fully cleanse our hearts, inward sin (unloving passions and affections) remains and we are in need of continual justification.

It is also important to note that Wesley insisted he did not think perfection was "sinless." Christian perfection as he understood it did not eliminate infirmities, mistakes, or temptation. Even though he trusted that God gave us power to resist sin, Wesley also realized that without intending to do so we could make a mistake that violates God's perfect law. We would never, then, be without the need for the atoning blood of Jesus Christ.

Mark Ellingsen asks a pastoral question: "But what do Methodists do when their expectations are not met, when holiness or good works do not happen in the lives of the faithful?" I am not sure whether this question is about no growth at all (which might require some exploration of giving one's heart to God) or about full deliverance from sin. On a practical level, I do not think many Methodists nowadays are led to expect a full deliverance from sin, so I have never encountered this situation. If I did, I might offer the solace expressed in a poem by Charles Wesley: "We believe, and rest secure, Thine utmost promises to prove, To rise restored, and thoroughly pure, In all thine image of Thy love, Filled with the glorious life unknown, For ever sanctified in one."

X. THE BLACK CHURCH TRADITION
FARRIS BLOUNT

A Tale of Many Options: Following Jesus in the Black Church Tradition

As many of my colleagues have noted during this series on following Jesus from diverse Christian traditions, there is no uniform structure or pattern to such a task. Following Jesus is primarily informed by the context of a people and the needs, desires, and goals of that people. This reality remains true within the Black Church tradition. As C. Eric Lincoln and Lawrence H. Mamiya write in their groundbreaking book, *The Black Church in the African American Experience*, "Black churches are institutions that are involved in a constant series of dialectical tensions." The theological emphasis of Black congregations, and therefore Black Christians' understandings and expressions of following Jesus, have sometimes shifted over time depending on the social environment. While some in the Black Church tradition have primarily highlighted how following

Jesus prepares us for life after death, others have been more focused on how Jesus models how we should be concerned with social concerns here and now (a dialectical tension that Lincoln and Mamiya call "other-worldly versus this-worldly"). These tensions still remain, because although people might believe that following Jesus in the Black Church tradition can largely be defined by a historical belief in and commitment to the freedom and liberation of all those who have been oppressed, there are still others in this tradition that would suggest being a disciple of Jesus is chiefly about one's individual salvation.

To begin, it is important to note that there is no such thing as the monolithic "Black Church." We often talk about the "Black Church" using this singular phrase, but if we are not careful, we run the risk of reducing or ignoring the complexities inherent across these institutions. Throughout this series, we have written about following Jesus from various Christian denominational traditions, but in some of the discussions, there is arguably a unique Black Church experience that adds further nuance to the conversation. There are, of course, Black Baptist congregations. But there are also Black churches in the Wesleyan tradition and Black parishes that identify with the Roman Catholic church. There are African-Americans who have their own experiences within the Anglican tradition. I believe, therefore, that to articulate what it means to follow Jesus in the Black Church tradition is a monumental task, because one must recognize that Black Christians can have such varied interpretations of such a topic due to our diverse denominational affiliations *and* our experiences of being Black in the world. For instance, some African-American Methodists most certainly would agree with various points made in the Methodist reflection due to their shared denominational identity. And yet those same individuals might con-

THE BLACK CHURCH TRADITION

tend that their social location as Black people in America, who must deal with racism and discrimination even in their congregational life, creates alternative understandings of what it means to follow Jesus.

In fact, the historical mistreatment and marginalization of African-Americans can explain how many Black Jesus-followers have understood that to follow Jesus means working toward the liberation of all those who are oppressed, particularly Black people. Such a perspective has been molded first by our historical experiences. Our Black Christian forebearers could not understand how a loving and redeeming Savior, who sought to restore our relationship with God and free us from the penalty of sin through his crucifixion, could support the brutal institution of American slavery. Throughout history, African-American believers could not make sense of how some people could worship a God on Sunday that made humankind in God's image and declared that this creation was good (Genesis 1) but then on Monday treat Black people like second-class citizens unworthy of rights and resources. Because of these realities, Black Christians have argued that the Jesus we serve laments with us as we process through the trauma that racism creates and fights alongside us as we work to create a world where all God's creation can thrive. In Jesus, we see someone who is our kin, as he lived as a minority under Roman oppression and constant threat of retaliation, ultimately resulting in his death at the hands of the state.

As one might be able to tell from above statements, the Bible is also a critical component to how we in the Black Church tradition understand following Jesus means working for the liberation of all those who are imprisoned by the "isms" (racism, sexism, etc.) preventing them from living the abundant life Jesus desires for all of us. Black Christians hold a high respect for the Bible; the majority, if not all, of Black churches will reference multiple Old or New Testament texts during our worship services. As our ancestors pushed for slave emancipation, the liberating ethos of the Exodus narrative was a rallying cry. During the Civil Rights Movement, the words of what has been called Jesus' inaugural sermon in Luke 4 rang through many a Black Church as pastors and faith leaders galvanized people, Christian or otherwise, to "proclaim good news to the poor" and "set the oppressed free." African-American followers of Jesus read, recite, and preach biblical texts that demonstrate how Jesus spent time with and healed those whom society had rejected as an indication of his condemnation of discrimination against any people group. The Bible then is a guidebook that instructs Black Christians on how to model Jesus' own ministry of compassion, liberation, and freedom.

The Black Church's commitment to justice and equality is not only historical; I have seen firsthand how countless Black congregations embody the belief that following Jesus translates into an active effort to challenge discriminatory policies and practices here and now. I currently attend a Black church in which the leadership and many of the members participated in protests following the murder of George Floyd in May 2020. My church has a social justice committee that facilitates opportunities to learn about local efforts to combat economic inequality, police brutality, and housing discrimination. In fact, in the immediate aftermath of George Floyd's death, my congregation partnered with a White Jewish congregation as we examined Isabel Wilkerson's book *Caste* and investigated how race has contributed to the creation of a caste system in America that forces non-Whites to the bottom of the social, economic, and political ladder. As I consider the national landscape of Black congregations, some are working to address food in-

THE BLACK CHURCH TRADITION

security in Black communities while others are finding ways to pay down the obscene medical debt that disproportionately impacts Black Americans, making it hard for many of us to access basic necessities. Still other Black churches are embracing the literal words of Jesus' sermon in Luke 4 and advocating to "set the oppressed free" from misdemeanor marijuana drug convictions in jurisdictions where the use of marijuana has now been legalized. These examples are not exhaustive but are meant to illustrate that Black churches across this nation define following Jesus as a call to fight for those who are taken advantage of or disregarded at every stage of life.

However, despite the myriad ways in which the Black Church tradition echoes this commitment to justice in following Jesus, such a commitment does not reverberate through the halls of every Black congregation. In fact, the disagreement about how African-Americans should respond to discrimination can be explored through a polarity that Lincoln and Mamiya call "the communal and the privatistic." If striving for equal and fair treatment of Black Americans in all areas of life is considered a "communal" approach to the Black Church tradition, then the privatistic approach is one in which there is a "withdrawal from the concerns of the larger community to a focus on meeting only the religious needs of its adherents." While the communal approach advocates echo that following Jesus involves active engagement against oppression, the privatistic approach proponents contend that following Jesus is all about an individual public declaration of belief in him and a resulting shift in behavior (e.g., no cheating, stealing, etc.). Communal believers see Jesus as a liberator who desires for us to experience some heaven on earth right now through just relationships and equitable policies, while privatistic believers see Jesus as someone who came chiefly to liberate us from sin and its penalty—eternal separation from God.[1]

FOLLOWING JESUS

In other words, there are some Black congregations that believe following Jesus has little, if anything, to do with justice but rather living a pietistic and morally upright life. These Jesus-followers are not at the front of the protest line or advocating for better healthcare treatment for Black mothers. Instead, their emphasis is on developing consistent spiritual practices that demonstrate their commitment to Jesus as their Lord and Savior. These believers will normally focus more on what God is sharing with them about their job, their dreams and aspirations, and their personal relationship with God than what God might be saying about our modern injustices and their responsibility in addressing them. For some Black Christians then, following Jesus in the Black Church tradition could be defined by using some of the same words in my colleagues' reflections.

To be clear, I am not condemning such an approach to following Jesus. On the one hand, there are spiritual practices, such as prayer and Scripture reading, that should undergird the life of a believer, no matter what one believes about how to follow Jesus. These practices give us the strength to keep serving and following Jesus amid life's difficulties. On the other hand, Black Christians who have dedicated themselves to fighting for justice have sometimes done so at tremendous personal sacrifice. Some have lost their jobs, families, and even their lives. Contrary to popular belief of the media's portrayal of the Civil Rights Movement, many Black congregations chose not to participate openly, if at all, in the movement out of fear of retaliation from the Ku Klux Klan and others who rejected African-American demands for equality. Even Jesus himself suffered at the hands of the state as he worked to upend social structures that marginalized women and the poor. In other words, if we in the Black Church tradition articulate that following Jesus is also a call to speak out against oppression, then we must name the significant risks at stake.

However, I do not believe we can avoid the fact that Jesus was a social revolutionary if we look at the Scriptures and his engagement in his world. And if that is the case, we in the Black Church tradition who call ourselves Christians and attempt to model the life of Jesus must ask ourselves: What am I willing to sacrifice and give up to follow the Jesus who came to give humanity life, and life more abundantly, right here and right now?

I realize these are generalizations—no one person falls into one camp and never oscillates between the two. However, this framework is meant to show that although many Black congregations believe fighting for justice is critical to following Jesus, others do not and choose to focus primarily on living a pietistic life to follow Jesus.

Highlights of Responses from Other Christian Traditions

BEING "OTHER-WORLDLY" OR "THIS-WORLDLY": A false choice keeps emerging in our conversations. Farris Blount, our Black Church CP, notes the tension between Christians either being "other-worldly" or being "this-worldly." Those Black Christians who have an other-worldly focus believe that "being a disciple of Jesus is chiefly about one's individual salvation that assures being in the presence of God some day in the future." In sharp contrast, Black Christians at the other pole believe that Christians should "have social concerns here and now"—"fighting for justice is critical to following Jesus."

Another way to describe this polarity is to note the tension between either being "communal" ("striving [together] for equal and fair treatment of Black Americans in in all areas of life") or being "privatistic" ("withdrawal from the concerns of the larger [human] community to a focus on meeting only the religious needs of . . . the adherents [of the Black Church tradition]."

Blount summarizes by asserting that "although many Black congregations believe in fighting for justice, others do not," choosing, rather, to "focus on the private experience of personal salvation." But, as I will never tire of saying, this is a false choice. It is both/and, not either/or.

But the conversation with Farris adds a new dimension to the past conversations about this false choice: consideration of the "sources" of these two poles. Why do Black Christians gravitate to one pole or the other?

Answering this question takes us back to an observation made by Terry Todd, our Pentecostal CP: "Following Jesus is primarily informed by the context of a people and the needs, desires, and goals of that people." In my own words, what deeply informs your beliefs about what it means to follow Jesus is "who you are," which includes the particularities of your "social location," such as your gender, race and ethnicity, socio-economic status, and sexual orientation, as well as "your story": the experiences you have had during your personal pilgrimage.

Farris elaborates on this deep influence of "who you are" for those who worship in the Black Church as follows: "One of the factors that creates diversity in the Black Church about what it means to follow Jesus [there is no monolithic Black Church]" is "our experiences of being Black in the world." Simply put, "the experiences of some Black Christians lead them to be strong advocates for social justice, and the experiences of other Black Christians lead them to a privatistic personal relationship with Jesus."

A few of our other CPs echo Farris. David Gushee, our Baptist CP, says that "Perhaps it was inevitable that after 400 years of systematic oppression in this country some African Americans would develop versions of Christianity that turned private and other-worldly." More pointedly, Wesley Granberg-Michaelson, our Reformed CP, observes that "The privatistic, other-worldly expressions of faith in the Black Church did not take root in a vacuum. That version of faith was taught by their white masters and their missionary collaborators so that they might be 'more accepting of their bondage.'"

In contrast, Farris observes that "The historical mistreatment and marginalization of African-Americans can explain how many Black Jesus-followers have understood that to follow Jesus means working toward the liberation of all those who are oppressed, particularly Black people." Farris adds that because "we cannot avoid the fact that Jesus was a social revolutionary," there is a movement within the Black Church (and in other traditions, as attested to by other CPs) "toward a focus on advocating for social justice."

While Farris expresses commitment to the "this worldly" strand in the Black Church, he is careful to "not condemn" the Black Christians who "turn to practices such as prayer and Scripture reading, not to invigorate them in the quest for justice, but rather to help them weather the harsh realities of being Black."

Hopefully, the above narrative will help white Christians, like me, to better understand the tensions experienced by Black Christians in contemporary America and the pain that many of them have experienced from many years of mistreatment and marginalization of Black Americans. But this raises the unanswered question as to whether we white Americans will decide to take steps to join together with Black Americans in their quest for social justice.

YOU MAY DECIDE TO HELP ME ONLY IF YOU FEEL MY PAIN: I dare to suggest that while understanding the struggles of Black Americans to realize social justice is necessary, it is not sufficient to motivate the vast majority of white Christians, including me, to join together with Black Christians by taking concrete actions that will foster social justice for all Black Americans. Just "understanding" the problem is not enough motivation. We white Americans must "feel" the trauma experienced by many Black Americans.

Michael King, our Anabaptist CP, suggests that it is difficult for white Americans to "feel" the depths of that pain: "I imagine beyond a certain point I can't grasp the depths of trauma intertwined with slavery and racism persisting both in historical memory and still so actively inflicted [on Black people] today."

How can we begin to feel that pain? By developing a "personal relationship" with our Black neighbors; and this will require that we take the time needed to "get to know them."

Questions for Future Conversations

Q1: Do you believe that being either "other-worldly" or "this-worldly" is a false choice? If so, how do you create a balance between these two poles?

Q2: Is it your experience that when you have a personal relationship with someone who is in pain, you will be more likely to do something to alleviate that pain?

Q3: What steps have you taken, if any, to develop personal

relationships with members of the Black Church who are experiencing social injustice? If not, what possible steps can you envision taking?

In It for the Long Haul

When reflecting on my colleagues' responses to my original post, I appreciate their thoughtful and insightful perspectives regarding the complexities I attempted to name when exploring what it means to follow Jesus in the Black Church tradition. I was grateful for their attention to what I know to be true but failed to examine adequately in my initial comments—the need for spiritual practices that sustain the follower of Jesus as she pursues the call of justice. I am ending this month's discussion with a sincere desire to create spaces within the Black Church that enable people to develop routines that strengthen their capacity to remain committed to the work of Jesus, in the same manner that our Savior modeled in his own life.

Several of my colleagues raised significant points in their writings, which highlighted some of the spiritual rituals that are primary characteristics of what it means to be a disciple of Jesus. In his response, Ellingsen noted that my reflection "did not address how worship and the sacraments facilitate following Jesus." He makes an excellent point, as even Jesus himself demonstrated how worship (through prayer) and the Eucharist can alert us to the presence of God and God's desire for us in the world. These practices can encourage us to be faithful to the call of God in our lives, even when it appears that God is requiring us to do something that is beyond our capacity, ability, or even desire. As Jesus is headed toward the cross in the ultimate act of obedience in his life, it is arguably his quiet time with God that gives him the strength to follow through with his life mission. Even amid his efforts to challenge oppression and proclaim good news to the disenfranchised, Jesus found time to seek God, hear from and receive wisdom from God, and refill himself in his commitment to justice. Jesus knew that he had to be connected to God if he had any hope of staying faithful to his assignment on earth.

Likewise, I must always remind myself that followers of Jesus can't expect to be in the fight for justice for the long haul if we do not find and engage resources that give life to the spirit of God that resides in each of us. There is an ever-growing number of people, organizations, and institutions that reject any effort to make this world a more just and equitable place. It can be exhausting when followers of Jesus who care that *all* of God's creation live abundant lives are in constant conflict with so many who choose to discriminate against certain populations. Such statements are even more significant when I consider Gushee's comment when, after writing about the systemic oppression African-Americans have faced for centuries, he notes, "[A]fter all, when you can do little to control what others do to you, maybe you focus on what you can do for yourself and what God will do for you now and in the life to come." I can't blame those followers of Jesus in the Black Church tradition who turn to practices such as prayer and scripture reading, not to invigorate them in the quest for justice, but rather to help them weather the harsh realities of being Black. When you "can do little to control what others do to you," which has been the prevailing narrative for Black Americans throughout history, you might take solace in the fact that you have access to a personal relationship with God that can give you hope to keep living day by day until you see eternity.

However, I also see, through the life of Jesus, tremendous value in engaging in worship, prayer, and meditation, as each is a life-giving tool in the journey toward justice. There is a reason why individuals such as Howard Thurman were so intent on emphasizing the inner life and care of the soul—they knew that if one could deeply know and experience God, she could increase the likelihood of gaining the fortitude required to persist in her push for social justice. It is these (sometimes) taken-for-granted practices that can refocus our attention on Jesus, the one who can provide us with what we need to keep challenging oppressive structures and discriminatory policies. Jesus is, as the writer of the letter to the Hebrews declares, "the author and finisher of our faith"—he is the one that upholds us when the "isms" of life threaten to suffocate our very lives. Therefore, I will leave this month's conversation with a renewed understanding that to be a follower of Jesus not only means embodying an unrelenting commitment to justice but also a dogged determination to engage in spiritual practices that will refuel, energize, and stabilize us as we pursue this justice.

XI. THE LATTER-DAY SAINTS TRADITION
ROBERT MILLET

Walking in His Steps: How Latter-day Saints Seek to Follow Jesus

It is not difficult for persons who have received academic training in such fields as Christian history, theology, or religious studies to lose their focus on the fundamental purpose of Scripture itself—to come to know God and Jesus Christ (John 17:3). The Apostle Paul expressed such a concern in his second letter to the Corinthians: "I'm afraid that your minds may be corrupted from the single-mindedness and purity which the Messiah's people should have" (N. T. Wright, The Kingdom New Testament). This is why I have enjoyed so much being a part of this dialogue: The focus is on what we do, in our respective traditions, to follow Jesus. In this essay I hope to be able to express what members of The Church of Jesus Christ of Latter-day Saints have been counseled to do in order to follow the son of God and thereby come to know him.

I begin with what Latter-day Saints are probably charged to do most often by church leaders—to *search the Scriptures daily* as individuals and as a family, to speak of them and teach them to one another. There is a power inherent in Scripture, a power unlike anything else we may read or study. Lew Wallace's *Ben Hur* makes for fascinating reading (and a pretty fair movie as well), but it cannot stir the soul like Isaiah 53 or the 23rd Psalm. Reading Lloyd C. Douglas's *The Robe* is a sweet experience, but its influence and impact are nowhere near what one can encounter in the Gospel of John. God has placed his seal of approval on Scripture, and as Paul taught, it is spirit-breathed (2 Timothy 3:16). The current President of our Church, Russell M. Nelson, pointed out that "To reach our objective of eternal life, we need to follow teachings . . . received from prophets of God. . . . In our journey through life, you meet many obstacles and make some mistakes. Scriptural guidance helps you to recognize error and make the necessary correction. You stop going in the wrong direction. You carefully study the scriptural roadmap."

Second, Latter-day Saints are a *praying* people. Indeed, we believe that no one can come to know Christ and acquire a Christlike nature unless they regularly and consistently offer up their petitions and their gratitude in prayer. Members of the Church are encouraged to have personal prayer in the morning and before retiring to bed, as well as having a prayer in our hearts throughout the day. We are counseled to gather our family around us in the morning and the evening to kneel in family prayer.

For us, prayers are not merely a time to make requests of the Almighty, but also a time to receive personal guidance from God. In particular, when an individual is in the process of making a very significant decision, he or she is encouraged to lift up their voices in prayer but then to remain on their knees for a while to "listen" for how God may choose to prompt or guide one's thoughts or feelings. One of the most beloved hymns in the Church's hymnal is "Ere You Left Your Room This Morning, Did You Think to Pray?"

Third, Latter-day Saints seek to follow Jesus by *serving and loving others* as he did. That is, we strive to walk in his steps (1 Peter 2:21). Jesus came to earth to carry out both his mission and his ministry. When I refer to his *mission*, I have in mind those matters to which only he could attend—redemption from sin and resurrection from death. The *ministry* of Jesus pertains to how he dealt with people—how he led them, loved them, lifted them, liberated them, and lightened their burdens. And it is the ministry of Jesus that we can in fact emulate. He put people first, and so can we. He was willing to be inconvenienced, and so can we. He reached out to those on the margins of society, and so can we.

In a rather comprehensive overview of what our Lord and Master did, Matthew wrote: "And Jesus went about all Galilee, *teaching* in their synagogues, and *preaching* the gospel of the kingdom, and *healing* all manner of sickness, and all manner of disease among the people" (Matthew 4:23; emphasis added; see also 9:35). In speaking of those who are called to teach the gospel, especially the youth, one Latter-day Saint leader, Jeffrey R. Holland, stated: "I do believe that Christ wants our teaching to lead to healing of the spiritual kind. . . As with the Master, wouldn't it be wonderful to measure the success of your teaching by the healing that takes place in the lives of your students?"

Holland continues, "Let me be a little more specific. Rather than just giving a lesson, please try a little harder to help that blind basketball star really see, or the deaf homecoming queen really hear, or the privately lame student body president really walk. Try a little harder to fortify someone so powerfully that whatever temptation the devils of hell throw at her or him, these students will be able to withstand and thus truly in that moment be free from evil. Can you try a little harder to teach so powerfully and so spiritually that you can take that student—that boy or girl who walks alone to school and from school, who sits alone in the lunchroom, who has never had a date, who is the brunt of every joke, who weeps in the darkest night—can you unleash the power in the Scriptures and the power in the gospel and 'cleanse' that leper, a leper not of his or her making, a leper made by those on our right and on our left and sometimes by us?" People matter, very much. God and Christ are in the "business" of people, and so must we be if we are to follow where Jesus leads.

I am personally very concerned, as I know each of you are, about the enormous exodus from faith that has taken place within the last decade or so—the purported 27% of the American population who have chosen to cut all ties with organized religion. These "nones," who speak of themselves as being "spiritual but not religious," often say that they do not find religion to be relevant to them. Others, especially young adults who have left the faith, have expressed to me how weary they are of the theological battles, the name-calling, the ever-present tendency to draw lines in the sand, to belittle, to exclude, to render harsh judgments against those who may believe differently. In so doing, we have given Christianity a bad name and demonstrated attitudes and behavior that are anything but Christian. There is a great need for a kinder, gentler form of Christianity, the kind that Jesus Christ displayed so beautifully.

Fourth, Latter-day Saints are deeply committed to the value of *church attendance*, of meeting together with "the body of

Christ." We need the Church. What takes place within the Church, and what takes place within each of us as we become enthusiastically involved in the Church, is essential in keeping ourselves "unspotted from the world" (James 1:27); it is a vital part of coming unto that perfection of the soul for which all followers of the Savior strive. Christianity entails more than prayer, fasting, and searching the Scriptures—more than an individual effort to live the principles of the gospel of Jesus Christ. As vital as personal devotion and individual effort are, Christianity is fully lived out only *in community*. God designed, for example, that the various offices of the Church of Jesus Christ had been put in place "for the perfecting of the saints, for the work of the ministry, for the edifying of the body of Christ: till we all come in the unity of the faith, and of the knowledge of the son of God, unto a perfect man [or woman], unto the measure of the stature of the fullness of Christ" (Ephesians 4:12-13). In short, the Church is given to assist and empower us toward that spiritual maturity that is the perfection of which the Scriptures speak.

Each Sabbath Latter-day Saints come to church and partake of the sacrament of the Lord's Supper. We do so in remembrance of the life and mission of Our Master, Jesus Christ. More specifically, we partake of the sacred emblems in remembrance of his bruised and broken body and his spilled blood on the cross. We believe and teach that if an individual comes to sacrament meeting (our main worship service) in a spirit of humility and repentance, that he or she can, through the ordinance of the sacrament, experience a remission of sins and enjoy the peace that accompanies the presence of the Holy Spirit. Sermons or spiritual messages that are delivered in our worship service help us learn or be reminded of the principles of the gospel of Jesus Christ. Singing the hymns and great anthems of praise lift our souls heavenward like nothing else that we might do.

Without the Church, one cannot develop those Christlike qualities and attributes that come only through association and affiliation with other men and women, boys and girls, who are striving for basically the same things we are. Nor can one participate in the ongoing service and organized sacrifice that come through working closely with others. Without the Church and church affiliation and involvement, one simply cannot cultivate the gospel light that emanates freely and enticingly from those who are on the path to life eternal.

"Since Jesus is at the very center of it all," one of our Church leaders observed, "*we must make him and his ways the light by which we steer and the light we hold up to others*. To proceed in any other way is to proceed with less light—much less light." It is the sweet labor of a lifetime to learn how to place the Savior at the center of our lives and to keep him there. As we look more consistently and reverently to him as the captain of our souls and our salvation, we discover the abundant life that he alone can give (John 10:10). That abundant life *here* is but a foretaste of the eternal life that awaits us *hereafter*.

Highlights of Responses from Other Christian Traditions

A NEAR-CONSENSUS ABOUT WHAT IT MEANS TO FOLLOW JESUS: One of our twelve CPs proposes the following overarching framework for how Christians should follow Jesus (slightly paraphrased):

We are committed to searching Scriptures as individuals and in collective settings, always striving for a better understanding of truth.

THE LATTER-DAY SAINTS TRADITION

We are committed to being a praying people, consistently offering to God our petitions and our gratitude for God's grace.

We seek to follow Jesus by loving and serving others as he did.

We seek to fully live out our Christian faith in community with other members of the Body of Christ.

Most of our other CPs view the above proposal as a "near-consensus" as to what it means to follow Jesus (with only two CPs expressing some reservations).

Surprise! The above overarching framework was proposed by Robert Millet, a member of the Church of Jesus Christ of Latter-day Saints (hereafter referred to as LDS), one of the various strands of Mormonism (which, as in most Christian traditions, range from "liberal" to "conservative").

This is a surprise because as you read in my introductory chapter some Christians questioned my including Mormons in this ecumenical conversation among Christians: "Is Mormonism really a Christian tradition?" I included them because Mormons identify themselves as members of a Christian tradition.

A first lesson to be learned is that if someone tells you that they are a follower of Jesus, and you do not believe that, the approach you should not take is to silence them, or, worse yet, demonize them. Rather, you should ask them to help you to better understand the ways in which they aspire to follow Jesus.

To start out with this question is to exemplify a "kinder and gentler" Christianity that Millet calls for in response to those who have left the Christian faith ("especially young adults"), who have told him "how weary they are of the theological battles, the name-calling, the ever-present tendency to draw lines in the sand, to belittle, to exclude, to render harsh judgments against those who may believe differently."

While the majority of the CPs expressed agreement with what Robert Millet said about the overarching framework for following Jesus that LDS members embrace, very significant concerns were expressed about issues that he did not address.

To cite just a few examples noted by some other CPs, Robert said nothing about the significant role that LDS Christians give to the *Book of Mormon* and the relationship between the *Book of Mormon* and the Bible, or the LDS belief that "the Canon of Scripture is open, flexible and expanding." He also says nothing about the apparent LDS non-acceptance of the post-New Testament creeds and theological formulations, including the doctrine of the Trinity.

Terry Todd, our Pentecostal CP, also expresses concern that Robert has reported on the LDS beliefs held by their leaders rather than from the rank-and file members, wondering "what might change if in our understanding [of LDS beliefs] if Dr. Millet had included other voices from the LDS—from the grassroots up, from the margins toward the middle, rather than exclusively from the leadership down." It is obvious that further conversations about these unresolved issues are needed, but with a "difference."

ONGOING CONVERSATIONS WITH A DIFFERENCE: Wesley Granberg-Michaelson, our Reformed CP, after expressing his concern about the issues that Robert Millet did not address, calls for future conversations about these issues but with a huge "difference": "Today, the honest and earnest discussion of these differences [regarding some LDS beliefs that Robert did not address] should take place as partners in a common faith, rather than as combatants."

And, from my perspective, the reason these future conversations can "take place as partners in a common faith, rather than as combatants" is the way in which our CPs engaged Robert Millet regarding LDS beliefs. From the start, rather than demeaning or demonizing LDS persons, they sought to understand their beliefs and the reasons they have for holding to those beliefs. This strategy did not resolve all disagreements. But it laid the foundation for continuing the conversation as partners rather than as combatants.

This perspective of mine points to the importance of the second purpose of this book, as stated in my introductory chapter: To provide a much-needed resource toward the goal of "continuing the conversation" by posing questions that were raised and unanswered in the initial conversation reported on in this book.

Questions for Future Conversations

Q1: Do you agree with the overarching framework for how Christians should follow Jesus proposed by Robert Millet? If not, what would you change?

Q2: Have you interacted with persons who have left the Christian faith because of the nasty way in which some (many?) Christians engage with those who disagree with them? If so, what did you say to them? If you have not interacted with such persons in the past, what would you say if such a person showed up at your door tomorrow expressing that concern?

Q3: What do you think of the strategy of starting a conversation with a person who strongly disagrees with you by asking them to help you to better understand their contrary position and the reasons they have for their position, because that starting point lays a strong foundation for then discussing disagreements in a loving and respectful manner? Have you ever tried doing that, and, if so, what were the results? Does this potential strategy provide hope for overcoming, or, at least, diminishing the current nastiness that characterizes much public discourse.

What I Have Learned that My Fellow Latter-day Saints Ought to Know

When I was first approached by Harold Heie about the possibility of my involvement in an e-dialogue, "Respectful Conversations," I wondered if I would have the time and energy to do so given that I was already engaged in dialogue with Evangelicals and Nazarenes, and was a part of a Christian interfaith dialogue (eight of us) in Los Angeles. But when I learned that my friend Richard Mouw had recommended me, I felt that I should participate. And I am so grateful that I did. It has been a wonderful experience for me—expanding my understanding of other Christian groups' beliefs and practices, correcting my own misperceptions, and possibly helping others in some small way to better understand my beliefs and way of life. I am eager to express some things to my own people that I have either learned for the first time or had reaffirmed. Some of these are the following:

In spite of what many people through the years have accepted as fact, religion is an area that *can* be discussed and discussed seriously without dispute, rancor, or confrontation.

Interfaith dialogue can be helped along by a good dose of curiosity. Because we live in a world of immense diversity, we simply ought to be interested in what other people believe.

Through interfaith dialogue one not only learns a great deal

THE LATTER-DAY SAINTS TRADITION

about the other person's faith, but in the process may also learn a good bit about their own.

God continues to work through people of various religious traditions to accomplish his purposes.

The women and men with whom I have associated in this dialogue are followers of the Lord who want to do what they can to bless individuals and, in their own way, change the world.

Those who have participated in this dialogue manifest a deep and abiding sense not only of love and adoration, but of awe and wonder toward Jesus Christ our Savior. Latter-day Saints could be greatly blessed by seeking to understand and feel such abiding reverence for the grandeur and majesty of deity.

Not everyone out there dislikes the Latter-day Saints, and that in this group I have encountered God-loving and Christ-affirming persons who, while deeply committed to their own tradition, acknowledge goodness and Christian virtues wherever they may be found.

After having read and studied the comments of eleven other religious scholars or church leaders from Roman Catholic, Eastern Orthodox, and Protestant denominations, there are a number of beliefs or practices of my associates for which I feel, in the words of New Testament scholar Krister Stendahl, "holy envy." There is much that they believe and practice that I find both fascinating and deeply moving.

XII. THE PENTECOSTAL TRADITION
J. TERRY TODD

Following Jesus to the Altar: One Pentecostal's Reflections

Bearing the weight of a grief I couldn't name, one Sunday I *tarried at the altar*, a classical Pentecostal phrase that involves praying mightily for a divine encounter with the Holy Spirit. I stood, along with others, near the front of the worship space, my body enveloped by the band's percussive rhythms and the praise team's soaring vocals. *I, I've seen God do it, and I know / it's working out for me. / It's getting ready to happen.* The entire assembly chanted the song's refrain, again and again: *It's getting ready to happen, it's getting ready to happen.* I wasn't kneeling at a structure but standing, walking, rocking on my heels at the "altar," a space that in most Pentecostal settings encompasses the center front of the church, stage left and stage right as well.

My moments of tarrying, or waiting expectantly, involved both the fervent hope for a divine encounter with the Holy

Ghost, and a struggle with my willingness to surrender to the experience. And then it happened.

When you're filled with the Holy Spirit, there's an array of possible embodied expressions—raising hands, speaking (or singing) in tongues, shuddering or jerking, holy dancing, weeping, moaning, fainting, or being slain in the Spirit, which can put your body prone. (We sometimes call this, tongue-in-cheek, "floor duty.") I began to "run the aisles," as it's called in Pentecostal practice, sprinting clockwise around the room's periphery. I was in motion, yet somehow still "at the altar," within the space of encounter. I wept as I ran, conscious of the Spirit's presence and nearing the point of surrender: *I've seen God do it, and I know . . . it's working out for me.* My run ended moments later as my body crumpled at the center-front of the worship space, where many others, too, labored under the power of the Spirit. Some ended up, like me, on the floor, eyes closed, body shuddering, some speaking in tongues, others moaning deeply.

As I returned to waking consciousness, the deacons brought me water, and I sat up to drink it in the afterglow of this divine encounter. Bishop Levi then asked me in a whisper, "You got what you came for?" He meant not just the emotional catharsis but the meeting of the Holy Spirit.

What, for Pentecostals, does it mean to follow Jesus? And what do expressive embodied encounters like the one I've described have to do with following Jesus? What are the ethical implications of such encounters? Those are crucial questions, but first I want to tackle matters of definition and scope: What do we mean when we speak of Pentecostalism? What are the boundaries of this confusing category? Who does it include or exclude?

THE PENTECOSTAL TRADITION

As our year-long conversations have revealed, our respective traditions are diverse, even when that internal diversity is overlooked or suppressed. But the Pentecostal world resembles the nightmare scenarios of Reformation-era popes who fretted about the fragmentation of Christ's Body due to the anti-Roman revolts across Latin Christendom. Pentecostalism carries the spiritual DNA of sectarian Protestantism, with pronounced tendencies to splinter endlessly across countless vectors—doctrine and biblical interpretation, competing leadership styles—as well as around race, ethnicity, region, national origin, and matters regarding access to wealth and other resources.

Is it even possible to speak of a coherent Pentecostal tradition? Do we mean "classical Pentecostalism," a category that includes the Church of God in Christ (COGIC), the Assemblies of God, the Church of God (Cleveland, TN), the Church of God in Prophecy, the Apostolic Pentecostal Church, hundreds of smaller groups, and thousands of independent Pentecostal churches? Do we include charismatics in non-Pentecostal denominations? What about neo-charismatics? Neo-Pentecostals? What about Christians who belong to churches that fall between these categories? No wonder some scholars have taken up the umbrella term "renewalist" to describe movements of Christians that emphasize the work of the Holy Spirit.

There are certain common experiences shared by many, if not most, renewalist Christians—family resemblances within this thicket of diversity. One of these resemblances is the experience of worship as a *theater of divine encounter*, a space of intense emotion and intimacy where God meets us at the altar.

I came into Pentecostal faith after decades inside and at the margins of the Episcopal Church where the "altar" is an object made of wood, stone, or other material, set within a designated space called the chancel. In Anglican settings, as in Orthodox and Roman Catholic traditions, altars are also places of divine encounters, where Christians encounter God in the Eucharist.

Yet the Pentecostal altar is not just a place but a *space* within the assembly. To be sure, Pentecostal altars might include material objects such as a table or a prayer railing at the front of the worship space where the faithful kneel, but *as an experience*, the Pentecostal altar is more than that. The altar is the space where Pentecostals learn what it means to follow Jesus through encountering the empowering presence of the Holy Spirit. As the early Pentecostal leader William J. Seymour taught, the altar is where "the great Shekina of glory is continually burning and filling with heavenly light."

Renewalist praise music has much to say about the altar as a dynamic space of encounter. Take, for example, the Elevation Worship neo-charismatic ballad, "O Come to the Altar." The message is one of vulnerability, desire, confession, forgiveness, and the yearning for transformation: "Have you come to the end of yourself? / Do you thirst for a drink from the well? / Jesus is calling," ... "O Come to the altar / The Father's arms are open wide," "Bow down before him," "Bear the cross as you wait for the crown." The ballad is an old-school altar call dressed in new fashions, but God is calling these Christians not to a particular place, not to a table or a railing. Wherever in the assembly they're standing, arms uplifted in a pose of surrender, they are at the altar, at the space of divine encounter. In a moment like this, the Holy Spirit is present in subtler ways than in my own kinetic experience that I related earlier. You can see it in the arms gently raised, the flutter of an eyelid, the soft murmur of tongues-speech, the tilt of the head toward heaven, the tapping of the heart with the palm of one's hand.

In more classical Pentecostal style, the late Gospel singer LaShun Pace sings about the fire of the Holy Spirit in "Is Your All on the Altar": "You can only be blessed and have peace and sweet rest / when you yield him your body and soul," reminding the assembly that the altar is a place of expectation, waiting, a place of surrender and reception, before it becomes the place of transformation. The Spirit burns away sin and whatever pain and burden we bring to sacrifice upon the altar. (For Pace in that moment, it was the grief she carried from the recent loss of her daughter.)

As a theater of divine encounter, the Pentecostal (or renewalist) altar can be a "transgressive space," a term Gastón Espinoza has used to describe the altars at Azusa Street, the 1906 Los Angeles revivals that helped put the Pentecostal movement on the Christian map. As Espinoza argues, Azusa Street's altar was transgressive for many reasons, not just because of its intensely embodied practices but also because black, white, Latino, and Asian-American Christians gathered there. Together. Transgressive indeed, this race-mixing in Jim Crow America, and certainly one of the reasons the earliest Pentecostals were despised by the mainline white Protestant establishment. Azusa Street represented a fleeting but powerful moment of cross-racial comity, itself a sign of life.

The altar where I first experienced the baptism of the Holy Ghost is a transgressive space, which is why I use the provocative language of "flying the freak flag" to unabashedly embrace Pentecostal ideas and (especially?) *actions* that might puzzle or even repel others. The explosive global growth of renewalist versions of the faith continues unabated, yet I'm under no illusion that most American Christians will soon dance in the aisles, even though that's exactly what they do at Middle Church, one of the old Dutch Reformed Collegiate congregations in New York City, historically one of the least renewalist places one could imagine.

Neither in my experience nor in my conviction is being "filled with the Spirit" an end unto itself. It's nothing short of earth shattering—or should I say *ego* shattering?—that the indwelling of the Holy Ghost leads to self-transformation: God is now *within* me, or at least within my metaphorical heart! Personal transformation also holds within it the potential for the transformation of the Christian assembly, and indeed the community beyond. In other words, spiritual transformation can and should have real-world effects.

In a Pentecostal world of such bewildering variety, it's not surprising that there are disagreements aplenty about those real-world effects, as our present American moment demonstrates. Renewalist Christians have been among the most ardent proponents of the prosperity Gospel, and the most fervent supporters of Trumpist attacks on American democracy, racial equality, and gender and sexual justice.

Yet there are other Spirit-filled Christians who preach and practice a version of renewalism that is wildly different in terms of everyday ethics. For instance, my Pentecostal life is centered in communities affiliated with The Fellowship of Affirming Ministries (TFAM), a network of mostly queer and mostly black Christians described by the anthropologist Ellen Lewin in her recent book, *Filled with the Spirit*. TFAM has deep roots within the largest black Pentecostal denomination in the U.S., the Church of God in Christ (COGIC), in part because our founder, Bishop Yvette Flunder, emerged from that tradition. At the same time, the congregation I serve is also associated with the United Church of Christ (UCC), a mostly white liberal mainline (or *oldline?*) denomination where some local congregations—surprise!—are increasingly awakening to Spirit-filled worship. How queer is *that* context?!

This isn't the place to recount the history of how TFAM and other queer-positive groups emerged from classical Pentecostalism, but in shorthand: A Spirit-filled community of people rejected the demonization of gender non-conforming people and sexual minorities. They offered instead a vision of church as a place "where the edge gathers," as Bishop Flunder puts it, a place of radical inclusivity open to people whose churches had marginalized or expelled them.

Many renewalist Christians would regard the communities where I worship to be a wellspring of satanic rather than sanctified power. They'd be repulsed by doctrinal transgressions, no doubt, but what would likely rankle them most is that we understand gender diversity and sexual difference as God-given, precious, holy. Our praise and worship are a reversal of the experience of some who have endured the trauma of exorcisms—*out, foul spirits of homosexuality!*—and expulsion from churches and families.

Renewalist Christians are a Spirit-loving people, yet as Scripture tells us, it's imperative to test the spirits. What are the everyday ethics of Christians who claim the moniker *Pentecostal?* What is the fruit of the Holy Spirit? It's not running the aisles, speaking in tongues, or exhibiting other charisms at the altar, though these embodied experiences are, for some of us, harbingers of the Spirit's arrival. But they are certainly *not* what it means to follow Jesus. Paul's words to the fractious communities he addressed in Galatians gives us clues about how the apostle understood everyday Christian ethics:

But the fruit of the Spirit is love, joy, peace, forbearance, kindness, goodness, faithfulness, gentleness, and self-control. Against such things there is no law. Those who belong to Christ Jesus have crucified the flesh with its passions and desires. Since we live by the Spirit, let us keep in step with the Spirit. Let us not become conceited, provoking and envying each other.

At the altars of TFAM communities, here in the United States, in Kenya, Uganda, and the UK, I've witnessed my Spirit-anointed Bishop prophesy the coming of a third Pentecost, one more expansive than St. Paul's wildest dreams, more inclusive and transgressive than the second Pentecost at Azusa Street. The "fresh wind" of this Third Pentecost, Bishop Flunder says, is an invitation to all of God's people—*everyone*–to work together for the spiritual, emotional, and material flourishing of all people. After all, isn't that what love is?

Bishop sings it better than I can ever say it, in her sermonic riff on a classic Pentecostal praise song, "I Hear the Sound of Pentecost":

I need some people to believe with me . . . that the power of love is stronger than the power of hatred, and the power of peace is stronger than the power of war. And if you believe with me, and trust with me, our voices will connect, one person to another and another. . . . God is greater than the power of the enemy.

That prophecy makes me dance with joy at the altar, as I await this Third Pentecost, grateful for the radically relational pneumatology that undergirds it.

Somebody shout Hallelujah, please.

Highlights of Responses from Other Christian Traditions

A MARVELOUS ECSTATIC EXPERIENCE APPRECIATED: As has been observed for most, if not all, of the Christian traditions involved in this ecumenical conversation, Terry Todd, our Pentecostal CP, acknowledges that there exists a diversity of strands in his tradition, leading some scholars to use the term "renewalist" to describe the various movements of Christians that emphasize the work of the Holy Spirit. But he also notes that there are "family resemblances within this thicket of diversity" and "One of these resemblances is the experience of worship as a *theater of divine encounter*, a space of intense emotion and intimacy where God meets us at the altar." He describes his own experience of such divine encounter in his Pentecostal church as follows:

When you're filled with the Holy Spirit, there's an array of possible embodied expressions—raising hands, speaking (or singing) in tongues, shuddering or jerking, holy dancing, weeping, moaning, fainting, or being slain in the Spirit, which can put your body prone. (We sometimes call this, tongue-in-cheek, "floor duty.") I began to "run the aisles," as it's called in Pentecostal practice, sprinting clockwise around the room's periphery. I was in motion, yet somehow still "at the altar," within the space of encounter. I wept as I ran, conscious of the Spirit's presence and nearing the point of surrender: *I've seen God do it, and I know . . . it's working out for me.* My run ended moments later as my body crumpled at the center-front of the worship space, where many others, too, labored under the power of the Spirit. Some ended up, like me, on the floor, eyes closed, body shuddering, some speaking in tongues, others moaning deeply.

Many of our other CPs express deep appreciation for Terry Todd's description of his ecstatic experience in his Pentecostal church. The many shouts of "Hallelujah" in response to Todd's invitation to shout out those words are followed by reports by some of having had similar ecstatic experiences. But some CPs also point to a danger.

THE DANGER OF THE INSTITUTIONAL CHURCH DOMESTICATING THE GIFT OF THE SPIRIT: Michael King, after reporting on his own experience of manipulation at an altar call in an Anabaptist church camp, points out that whatever mysterious thing is taking place at the altar, the "meeting of the Holy Spirit" is a "gift" that cannot be coerced or controlled.

The institutional church finds this inability to control the results of such an encounter with the Holy Spirit to be threatening, especially when the result of such an experience leads a recipient of this gift into a "transgressive space" where he/she calls into question ethical and theological conclusions that differ from institutional commitments. Todd cites the example of the Fellowship of Affirming Ministries ((TFAM), to which he belongs, a network of "mostly queer and mostly black Christians" who "reject the demonization of gender non-conforming people and sexual minorities." This suggests the possibility that the results of such revised ethical and theological position are not self-authenticating; they must be "tested."

TESTING THE SPIRITS: Robert Millet, our LDS CP, poses the following question to Terry Todd: "How do members of your church discern what manifestation is from God, from man, or from the devil?" This question suggests the need to test novel ethical or theological claims. My own position relative to novel ethical claims is that any such claims must "pass the test" of not being destructive of one's understanding of Christian values.

THE CONCEIT OF MAKING MY CHRISTIAN EXPERIENCE NORMATIVE: While the various CPs (and I) allow for, and express deep appreciation for, the ecstatic experiences of many Christians within the Pentecostal tradition, and other Christian traditions, no CP (as well as I and Terry Todd) embraces the idea that such an experience should be normative for all Christians. A major conclusion emerging from our series of conversations is that there should be significant latitude in how Christians, within any tradition, decide to follow Jesus, provided, I would add, that such decisions do not lead to actions that are destructive of one's understanding of Christian values. But, what then, holds us together?

A SHARED COMMITMENT TO FOSTERING GOD'S REDEMPTIVE PURPOSES: My own conclusion to this ecumenical conversation is that what should hold us together in the midst of our diversity in beliefs about what it means to "follow Jesus" is our shared commitment to "partnering with God" in planting tiny "seeds of redemption" (see the parable of the Mustard Seed, as recorded in Matthew 13:31-32) in accordance with a personal ethic one has embraced (the set of value commitments that one understands to be foundational to the Christian faith and one's beliefs as to what actions either foster or are destructive of those values).

Questions for Future Conversation

Q1: Have you ever had the kind of ecstatic "divine encounter" that Terry Todd describes? If so, how would you describe your experience? If you have not experienced such an encounter, do you believe something is missing in your Christian experience?

Q2: Todd focuses on what he considers to be one possible work of the Holy Spirit in the life of a Christian. Does that possible work exhaust Christian teachings about the work of the Holy Spirit? If not, what is missing?

Q3: The biblical teachings about the critical importance of being characterized by the Fruits of the Holy Spirit (love, joy, peace, patience, kindness, generosity, faithfulness, and self-control—see Galatians 5:22-23) received scant attention in this conversation. Todd suggests that this is important for "everyday Christian ethics," but the other CPs do not comment on this assertion. Do you believe that is a shortcoming of our conversation? If you believe that is a shortcoming, what would you say to correct it?

Q4: Possibly the most meddlesome lesson I have learned from this twelve-month conversation is that it is a mistake for adherents to any Christian tradition to assert that the emphases within their particular tradition about what it means to follow Jesus should be the emphases within all Christian traditions. Do you agree with me that this is a mistake? If not, why not? If you agree with me, have you ever found yourself making that mistake?

Q5: Do you agree with my grand conclusion that what should hold us together as Christians in the midst of the great diversity in beliefs that have been expressed in this twelve-month conversation about what it means to "follow Jesus" is our shared commitment to "partnering with God" toward the realization of God's redemptive purposes by means of "planting tiny seeds of redemption"? If you do not agree with me, what is it that you believe should hold us together as brothers and sisters in Christ?

Following Jesus Is a Liquid Dance

As we conclude this year-long experiment in respectful conversations, I'm grateful for the ways my faithful beloveds have responded to the post about my adopted tradition, Pentecostalism. Throughout the *Following Jesus* conversations, I've

THE PENTECOSTAL TRADITION

been struck by how many posts have included stories, highlighting the *lived experience* of our respective traditions. This set of responses was no exception.

My story about the Pentecostal altar evoked *your* stories, many of them narratives about Holy Spirit encounters of one kind or another. My friend Randall Balmer wrote about a visit he and I made to an Apostolic (Jesus-only) Pentecostal Church in Natchez, Mississippi, decades ago, where we met Sister Ramsey. That was the first time I had witnessed a Christian being filled—*in that way, in that very moment, and before my eyes!*—with the Spirit. (Was it also your first time, Randy?) Raised fundamentalist, I was suspicious of Pentecostal charisms, which God withdrew (or so said my Calvinist elders) after the apostolic era. Balmer calls Sister Ramsey's spirit-filled moment "a liquid dance." That's a fascinating choice of words, and spot-on in describing my experience of the Holy Spirit. Spirit as fire, wind, vibration, breath, yes—yet liquid is also an apt metaphor. After all, the Holy Spirit *flows* through bodies and spaces in ways that can be gentle as a brook or fierce like a tsunami.

I wish I had more time to answer Bob Millet's question regarding my move from Anglican to Pentecostal paths. I have lots of stories about *that*. Yes, it's a dramatic departure, yet the conversion itself was slo-mo; it took years, although it began with seeing Sister Ramsey's fully embodied reception of the Spirit. Over the years, the Holy Spirit's lure became irresistible and took me to places I never expected to go. (Maybe *surprise* is a key element of the Spirit's M.O.?)

I was deeply moved by Michael King's story of Holy Ghost failure. When a wave of charismatic fervor swept his summer camp, skeptical Michael endured the entreaties of his friends at a prayer meeting—"just let go!"—so that he could receive what Pentecostals call the "evidence" of Spirit's presence—tongues-speech. Michael managed to blurt out some sound that could pass, but no life transformation ensued.

I've experienced incidents like this many times, and in my queer corner of the Pentecostal world, we sometimes laugh at the memory of our own earnest entreaties. But often it's not funny. Michael analyzes the scene memorably as "external coercion blending with my inner need," echoing the experience of many who've left Pentecostal communities to join the ranks of the *none* or *done*. They left because they experienced coercion and manipulation to the point of spiritual abuse at the hands of Pentecostal leaders who arrogantly suppose that *they* are the guardians of the Spirit's power.

Michael's story continues with deeply moving reflections on an enduring marriage with his wife, whose earlier charismatic encounters shaped her own spiritual life. They've settled into a loving partnership and into a quieter relationship with the Holy Spirit that Michael describes through reference to a Mennonite confession of faith, expressing a pneumatology that I can embrace wholeheartedly. No tongues required, no holy dancing, and no running the aisles necessary. Just relationship, *just* relationship, with God and with each other.

David Gushee relates a story about a moment of prayer with friends. At a time of personal anguish, he writes, their prayers evoked the Spirit's arrival, touching off moments of weeping for the suffering of others. In David's case, "the resentment in my heart toward a boss at work was quite simply and permanently burned out of me." That sounds like transformative healing to me, and it is one of the holy effects of worship in the assembly I serve. I'm grateful that you related that personal instance of the Spirit's manifestation, David. And I appreciate when you say that ". . . [such] experiences mainly seem frightening to me, in part because being that 'out of control' in public is almost the definition of terror to me." I've felt that terror, too, while witnessing the Spirit work. Opening to the Spirit requires a degree of naked vulnerability that I can rarely conjure in the presence of others.

Finally, David Ford offers up a story that begins at one of the citadels of American renewalism, Oral Roberts University, where he once studied. Then Ford takes us back to the second century, to the proto-Pentecostal movement known by its critics as Montanism and later condemned by an ecumenical council. Learning about Montanism was crucial to David's conversion to Orthodoxy. About the prophets Montanus, Priscilla, Maximilia, "I came to understand that there was *no way to control such a situation* [emphasis mine]; for who knew what they would prophesy next and make obligatory that would be contradictory to the Gospels and the letters of Paul."

This isn't the place to review the history of a much maligned and much misunderstood ancient Christian renewal movement. Maybe it's sufficient to say that the New Prophets, a group that included women as prophets and presbyters and possibly bishops, expressed dire concern about the growing tendency of the (male) episcopacy to arrogate for themselves the Spirit's power. Whatever their shortcomings, the New Prophets realized the world was groaning in pain under the weight of Roman imperial forces. The prophets called out a growing acquiescence among Christians to intolerable realities and called for repentance and renewal through a Holy Ghost revival. They dared to imagine the Spirit burning through principalities, powers, and a complacent church. No wonder some twentieth-century Pentecostals would come to identify with these ancients.

Ford sees the uncertainties as a frightening: "there was no way to control such a situation." David, you're exactly right: There *is* no way to control a situation where the Holy Spirit shows up. And as I see it, that's precisely the point. As John's Gospel tells us, "God's Spirit [wind] blows wherever it wishes. You hear its sound, but you don't know where it comes from or where it is going. It's the same with everyone who is born of the Spirit." I'm in awe of the Spirit's tendency to move in my heart as well as in the assembly, sometimes as a sirocco and sometimes as a sea breeze, to wake me up and blow away my complacencies, certainties, and pretensions.

Bob Millet asks about the mechanics of discernment in the assembly where I worship, how it is that we judge whether a manifestation is from God or signals something sinister. That's a crucial question for every community, and especially so for renewalists. The question requires a much longer response, but in shorthand . . . I've heard my Bishop answer it with Scripture: *From now on, beloveds, if anything is excellent and if anything is admirable, focus your thoughts on these things: all that is true, all that is holy, all that is just, all that is pure, all that is lovely, and all that is worthy of praise.* The trick is to know what those words mean in the contemporary *polis*, a question that will inevitability produce lots of argument among Christians. But that's another (related) story.

Every movement produces its charlatans; renewalism has conjured more than its share of fakers and frauds and abusers and those who've demonstrated an eagerness to offer incense to Caesar out of lust for power, a misplaced nostalgia for a vanished world, or some combination of both. We see these tendencies rampant in our own contemporary moment, requiring a sacred pause to test the S/spirits. That's why, in my original post, I recited from Galatians Paul's list of the Spirit's gifts: love, joy, peace, forbearance, kindness, goodness, faithfulness, gentleness, and self-control, what Blount in his response calls "the evidence that reveals our commitment to following Jesus."

Every single tradition represented in our respectful conversations carries shards of divine wisdom passed to us by our forebears, including wisdom about the Holy Spirit's *inspiration* of Christian life. That wisdom passes to us through imperfect institutions and their imperfect guardians and through butchers, bakers, candlestick makers, computer coders, and the people who clean offices and hotel rooms. Stories like the ones I've heard (and the ones I've told) throughout this year-long conversation remind me of the embodied and relational nature of Christian faith.

Our stories are also testaments to how we follow Jesus in certain places, in particular moments, and in communion with others *whose lives are closely linked with ours*, to cop a prayer book phrase. In other words, we live our commitment to following Jesus within communities shaped by circumstances. As you've heard me say several times in the past year, context is crucial and in a sense determinative. While I have a lot in common with the new prophets of the second century and even with their opponents, this is not the second century and there is no recapturing the primitive church.

As embodied souls we are here for *such a time as this*. Some of the roadblocks to the flourishing of *all* God's people are novel—a climate emergency on a global scale, the possibility of nuclear destruction, along with the usual human litany of greed, war, murder, inequality, and exploitation.

How do we sing the Lord's song in such a strange land? Well, it's not all dependent on our singing, thank God, since I can't carry a tune in a bucket. Maybe it's the Spirit that plays and sings through us. Glory! In a prophetic phrase attributed to Montanus, "Behold, the human being is like a lyre, and I [the Spirit] fly over them as a pick."

Breathe *that* in, trust, then open yourself to the "liquid dance."

XIII: Diversity and Blessing

JOHN G. STACKHOUSE JR.

Diversity has been a hallmark of Christianity since Jesus called Matthew to join his band alongside the fishermen he had previously taxed (and doubtless infuriated), and since our Lord befriended humble folk such as Mary, Martha, and Lazarus while dining frequently with the rich and influential. Only a few years later, the early Church divided—amicably, to be sure—into Jewish and Gentile communities (Acts 15), bound together in common loyalty to Jesus and willing to help each other financially, but also agreeing to differences (that would only increase) in liturgy and ethics.

Diversity today marks even communions that emphasize their comprehensive unity. Think of Roman Catholic worship in a Brazilian favela versus a mass in Notre-Dame. Consider the grandeur of a Church of England coronation service in Westminster Abbey versus an Alpha course not far away at Holy Trinity Brompton. Even the Orthodox's famous "Jesus

Prayer" comes in more than one version, and Orthodox unity has been sorely tried of late over Russia's invasion of Ukraine.

One of the key questions at the heart of this conversation is the legitimacy of diversity in the Christian Church and what the Lord wants us to do with it. Are we to mourn it as a travesty of Jesus' command to "be one" in the Last Supper Discourse (John 13-17)? Are we to celebrate it in the spirit of the multicultural festivities of the New Jerusalem (Revelation 21; cf. Isaiah 60)? Or are there other ways to think of and respond to the diversity of the Church?

It can help us think normatively about diversity and division (are they good things or bad?) by considering them historically. Much of the Church's diversity has been simply the consequence of evangelistic success. Different people, different *kinds* of people, come to Christ and bring with them all that they are. Converts literally speak different languages—with all the cultural difference that that implies. Converts come from up and down the social scale and have differences of education, employment, artistic taste, and so on. Diversity thus is a mark of God's blessing as God's kingdom advances.

Some diversity in church history has been fatally bad, to be sure, manifesting in heresy and schism. Such threats had to be dealt with by surgical division when all attempts at healing failed. With too much diversity, Christianity becomes something else: perhaps Gnosticism, perhaps moralism, perhaps lightly retouched Judaism—all of which were live options evident already in the New Testament. Other forms of diversity and division have arisen out of small- and narrow-mindedness, conceit, arrogance, intolerance, uncharity, and similar nasty traits so often warned against, again, already in the New Testament. Christians refused to accommodate each other, so preferring their own way of doing things as to split the fellowship. So, yes, wherever and whenever there is sin, there is the threat of unwarranted division, and faithful Christians must discern it and respond to it as the Bible teaches. I simply observe here that not all diversity is sinful.

Some of the participants in this book's conversation champion a particular way of celebrating the Eucharist as particularly enriching to them. One can only praise the Lord for such joy, even as one takes care not to imply that other forms are necessarily deficient. Two of the most moving communion services in my life took place in radically different situations: One in an ornate Anglican service brimming with smells, bells, and deeply textured music, and the other in the silence of a Sunday morning "breaking of bread" service among some Plymouth Brethren. The splendor of a rococo Catholic church might send one person off on transports of delight while bewildering or even repelling someone much more at home in the austere modesty of a Mennonite meeting house. Gregorian chant prompts one person to deep prayer while soothing another to mere slumber, and hard-driving gospel music lifts someone out of her seat in praise while her neighbor heads for the nearest exit. Some missionary situations require the oversight of a single capable leader wielding virtually monarchical authority (I think of nineteenth-century bishops having to care for huge areas in the western reaches of my native Canada) while other churches require a much more democratic approach to governance if they are to survive at all in a given culture (as has been true of virtually every denomination of Christianity in the United States).

Diversity, therefore, can simply be expected among a worldwide church full of different kinds of people. And division can be the result of any one of a number of historical events, from rulers seeking a rallying point for their subjects against a foreign threat (as the Dutch adopted Calvinism against the imperial Spanish Catholics) to splits in the American church over slaveholding, and from Scots arguing about who should have the final say in appointing clergy to African charismatics arguing over which apostles and prophets among them should govern the rest. Diversity and division can be good, bad, or unavoidably accidental, we might conclude.

What this book affirms is not that all diversity is evil, but that self-contented isolation is not a sensible Christian option in the face of our own evident deficits and the resources apparently available in other communities. To become all Christ wants us to be requires us to learn from different others, not simply become more and more what we already are.

For all the learning we can gain from each other, to be sure, we remain, and should remain, authentically ourselves. There is no single ideal form of Christianity that somehow combines all that is good in all the others into a coherent whole. We face inescapable and insurmountable finitude as individuals and as communities. Not even an *œuvre* as capacious as Bach's or Mozart's or Beethoven's can musically express the full range of human experience. Sometimes you need a symphony orchestra and sometimes you need a bluegrass band. A diet of only one or the other style of music leaves one significantly impoverished. But there is also just no way a single group even over multiple concerts can play all the music and say all that needs saying. The best we can hope for in transformative interactions with each other is to become better versions of ourselves. Pentecostals can learn from Presbyterians how to run good meetings while Presbyterians can learn to loosen up in worship from the Pentecostals. They can exchange excellent hymns. And both can learn something of grandeur in worship from the Catholics and Orthodox, while everyone

DIVERSITY AND BLESSING

can enjoy a little quiet with the Quakers. There is much to be gained in such earnest, open encounters, and I am glad our impresario, Harold Heie, has fostered them.

Early in this conversation, however, Brother Heie (to whom, in the following, I shall refer deferentially as "HH"), turns the discussion in an unexpected direction. Away from such longstanding Christian controversies as those over the nature of the Eucharist, the Latin mass, and the correct ethical use of the law in Scripture, HH asks his colleagues to discuss, of all things, sexual diversity in general and same-sex marriage (SSM) in particular.

Is HH looking for trouble? Why in the world bring up what the politicians call a "wedge issue"—indeed, what is arguably the most divisive ecclesiastical question of our time?

The logic of HH's move here, though, soon becomes clear. If we can learn from each other in conversation over such an incendiary matter as this, then surely other issues, even perhaps some stuck at longstanding impasses, can be broached. Fair enough, but I find myself compelled to offer what philosophers might call the complementary proposition: that failure in dialogue over this issue might also be instructive.

Is resolving conflict about SSM really a matter of listening, as HH hopefully suggests? "Listen to the stories of LGBTQ++ people," he pleads. This request is almost invariably raised in such conversations as the first step toward constructive interaction. For some decades now, however, this listening has taken place in several communions across North America. And what has happened?

I had a front-row seat in such a process in the Anglican Diocese of New Westminster, Vancouver. Under the direction of a determined bishop, the diocese undertook listening and group study and public discussion for over a decade. Let me make clear that the listening included attention to the poignant testimonies of people identifying themselves with sexual and gender minorities, testimonies offered by those people themselves as well as by others on their behalf, in large groups and small. The result of all this dialogue and listening? A very public lawsuit over church property litigated before the British Columbia Supreme Court that prompted a very public schism. This pattern of intramural listening, teaching, studying, and conversing that result in a bitter split has been repeated over and over across North America and is happening yet today in denominations on both sides of the Canadian/American border. Listening hasn't seemed to help. Why not?

I want to try to help here by identifying an intrinsic and inescapable problem. This problem doesn't entail that we stop listening to and learning from each other. But recognizing it will help us be realistic in our expectations of dialogue. In particular, it will keep us from attributing failures in dialogue necessarily to other people's lack of intelligence, sanctity, or good will. Instead, there might be an intractable problem that simply must be acknowledged and dealt with as positively as possible. And this problem is that of incommensurate styles of theology.

Elsewhere I have argued that there are only three main styles of modern Protestant Christianity in general, which I label "liberal," "evangelical," and "conservative." (A similar trio can be seen readily enough among Catholics and Orthodox, but a generally accepted term for the middle style in their circles is not apparent to me.) These three labels can easily be misunderstood, so let me explain immediately what I do *not* mean by them.

I am not referring to three kinds of politics, or three kinds of sexual ethics, or three kinds of worship services. In particular, I am not linking liberal theological method with left-wing ideologies nor evangelicals with the likes of Donald Trump. I am not linking conservatives with the alt-right—or, for that matter, with preferences for monarchy! There are lots of other legitimate uses of the terms "liberal," "evangelical," and "conservative."

In this conversation, I mean instead to refer strictly and only to *how* we construct our theology (and, thus, the ethical ramifications of our theology). And my contention here is that while individuals and communities within one of these three styles can profitably not only listen to each other, as HH wants Christians to do, but critically and constructively engage each other on matters of substance—members of one or another group cannot likewise engage those from the other styles. They cannot get very far theologically because they are using different operating systems, so to speak: different theological epistemologies.

Liberals can fairly easily listen to each other on a wide range of matters since they sit more or less loose to anything but their own fundamental convictions. Paradoxically, they can be quite fierce, one might even say "dogmatic," about core values: the priority of care for the poor and otherwise marginalized; the repellancy of doctrinal precision; dubiety about ecclesiastical authority; disgust in response to anything resembling church discipline; the inherent goodness of maximum inclusivity; and the centrality of God, however one understands him, her, or it. Liberal listening and learning across even quite thick and long-established lines of tradition (say, between Methodists and Presbyterians or even between Catholics and Protestants) is therefore not a terribly challenging enterprise. Why not? It's because the liberal is free (*liber* = "free") to choose as one likes among Scriptures, traditions, and the ideas and practices of the moment while blessing others who choose differently—so long as those others share that core regard for God, spiritual freedom, welcoming community, and social concern.

(May I say here in the interest of a fair hearing that I mean no disrespect to liberals. Indeed, I devoted myself to considerable study of liberal Christianity, and particularly of F. D. E. Scheiermacher, under the tutelage of two of the world's experts on these matters, Professors B. A. Gerrish and Langdon Gilkey of the University of Chicago. And I have traced the trajectories of liberal Christianity with some care in my native Canada as part of my historical scholarship. I apologize, however, if anything in my attempt to summarize complex matters in an accessible way comes across as pejorative.)

Beyond their own circles, moreover, liberals can enjoy a measure of mutually profitable dialogue with their evangelical and conservative counterparts. Liberals might remind their interlocutors of genuinely Christian values being currently overlooked or at least underplayed (such as social responsibility, as we have seen in this volume) while liberals in turn might pick up items from the others they may find valuable to add to their religious repertoire: songs from the Black churches, perhaps, or icons from the Orthodox. Indeed, when it comes to the means of grace, sacraments, spiritual disciplines, liturgies, prayers, artworks, and other aids to piety, Christians of all stripes have much to offer each other. The symbolic versatility of such practices and artifacts facilitates lending in a way that the specificity of doctrinal propositions and even ethical prescriptions often prevents.

Significant disputation, however, simply cannot take place—by which I mean argument that can actually change minds. This is so because the theological methods, the underlying epistemologies, are incommensurate. Put sharply, evangelicals and conservatives can argue with each other over the Bible, because they agree that it is the Word of God written—while the liberals are free to take Scripture or leave it as they see fit. Conservatives, for their part, can argue with each other over the tradition they hold sacred, with recognized authorities being vehemently invoked on one side or another—while both evangelicals and liberals stand by unmoved. Liberals, for their part, can argue with each other over their common values, even excommunicating each other for insufficient fidelity and fervor—while evangelicals and conservatives wonder why at least some liberals bother very much to retain the label "Christian" other than out of mere nostalgia, given the thinness of their allegiance to historic Christian affirmations.

(This is where I will register my surprise at the inclusion of the Church of Jesus Christ of Latter-day Saints in this discussion. I have enjoyed a friendly relationship with Bob Millett, toward whom I have considerable affection and regard, and he and I have lectured at each other's schools: Brigham Young University and Regent College. But the LDS Church is a strange mix of Christianity—one part Roman Catholic, in its powerful hierarchy and mysterious traditions; one part evangelical, in its global missionary career as part of its larger emphasis on lay ministry; and one part charismatic, in its fostering of immediate awareness of the Spirit as a "burning in the bosom"—and at least another three parts of truly outlandish teaching no other Christian church comes close to endorsing, from myths of Christ in the Americas to promises of interplanetary dominion. I recognize that not long ago in church history Catholics, Protestants, and Orthodox also excommunicated each other as simply not Christian, and in some parts of the world this harsh inhospitality continues. Still, at least at present, listening to Mormons for most Christians amounts to interreligious dialogue, not interdenominational discussion.)

I ruefully acknowledge that my contentions here will be unwelcome to many, if not all, of the participants in this project. But I believe HH's bold focus on same-sex marriage proves my point. Where has listening in fact done anything except move some individuals and congregations across the line of division, while the line remains and actual division results? Listening simply cannot accomplish very much if the underlying epistemology, the way of construing theology and ethics, isn't commensurate. Alas, I think this is a major reason why the kind of conversation HH desires simply cannot, and does not, take place. People of the highest intelligence and good will simply talk past each other, and we need to recognize why so as not to blame our conversation partners nor simply keep on in the same doomed dialogues.

And yet . . . ! HH, Wesley Granberg-Michaelsen, and others familiar with the Reformed tradition might worry that there is too much "antithesis" and not enough "common grace" in what I have said so far, let alone sufficient recognition of our common allegiance to Jesus. What about "one Lord, one faith, one baptism"?

I hastily proceed therefore to two kinds of reflections on commonalities that are evident in this book's discussion and that may be of some guidance in the future conversations we all hope will ensue. The first is a list of framing categories for conversations about "following Jesus." The second is a list of the several ways, not just two, in which we can profitably undertake such searching dialogues. I will then conclude with a few practical implications stemming from all this reflection.

Anyone engaged in the Christian education of inquirers and new believers faces the daunting task of formulating and then presenting a comprehensive, but simple, paradigm of Christian discipleship. Let's look at one such paradigm, which is comprised of two modes, two vocations, and four foci.

Among the glories of Christianity is its dual emphasis on the individual and on the community. Not all religions maintain such a balance. Daoism, for instance, is highly individualistic while Confucianism focuses on the community. Christianity, however, without ever specifying an *equal* balance, consistently speaks of the individual before God as a participant in the community of God's people. Any version of Christianity, therefore, that skews toward individualism to the neglect or derogation of the Church, on the one hand, or that valorizes the Church (the congregation, or denomination, or Church as a whole) at the expense of individual dignity, responsibility, and flourishing, on the other, is substandard Christianity and warrants remedy. Because individualism is such a driving force in American culture, thoughtful Christians often champion community as its antidote. Sometimes, however, such discussion becomes irresponsibly romantic as it overlooks the ways in which religious communities can foster pathologies ranging from doctrinal and ethical rigidity to domestic abuse. As one looks over the essays in this volume, therefore, one would do well to consider whether in each case an individual following of Jesus is nicely complemented by a corporate following and vice versa. Both modes matter.

As for God's call upon human beings, it comes in two forms. The original (Genesis 1 & 2) and permanent human calling is to join with God in cultivating shalom, in promoting universal flourishing. The term "cultural mandate" surfaces in such discussions, but it sometimes seems to be restricted to human work in and with the rest of creation. Instead, God's call in creation is literally global and all-encompassing: to love God with all one's heart, to love one's neighbour as oneself, to cooperate with God in one's own fulfilment, and to bless the rest of the world with skillful, compassionate, and creative care. This is what it means to "reign with Christ" in the world to come (2 Timothy 2:12). We are not to end up in heaven sitting on clouds playing harps in an endless church service. We are destined for Earth 2.0, as the new capital city of God's making, the New Jerusalem, comes down from heaven to a renewed planet on which the redeemed will dwell with God and continue the work of creativity the Creator created us to do at the first. Following Jesus thus means taking stock of who and what one is—and who and what *we* are, as any corporate entity (family, company, institution)—and then contributing all we can to the flourishing of God's world.

Alas, of course, the Bible informs us of the devastation of sin. God's second vocation comes, therefore, to Christians: the Great Commission to make disciples across the world (Matthew 28:18-20). Only by gladly coming into Jesus' personal orbit of influence, only by rebirth in his Spirit, and only by taking up his commandments and his cross in the company of his community can we find our way back to God and forward to the world to come. Thus, Christians take on this second, peculiar calling to the generic human calling of shalom-making.

It is precisely for the full realization of shalom on earth that Christians work diligently with the Spirit to bring men and women to conversion and then upward into the full life of God. Each Christian thus has at least one Spiritual gift to share with the rest of Christ's body in the Church's mission to draw people in, welcome them home, and grow them up into full maturity (Colossians 1:28). Following Jesus thus means taking stock of who and what one is—and who and what *we* are, as any corporate entity (family, congregation, denomination, special purpose group)—and contributing all we can to the salvation of God's world.

Here I must wonder out loud, with respect but also with some dismay, at the lack of attention paid to evangelism and disciple-making in this volume. When evangelism is mentioned at all, and only briefly, it is usually in terms of "what we need more than" or "what we must transcend"—as if the contemporary Church in all its branches is humming along well enough in evangelism and disciple-making and needs a reminder to engage in more and better social work or political action or cultural improvement. (Or is it something else? I detect an occasional hint that sophisticated, serious Christians should somehow "outgrow" evangelism and serve humanity in other ways. But for an organism thus to forego regeneration and reproduction is not sapient, but senescent.)

To take evangelism for granted strikes me as just factually wrong, at least for North America, Europe, and Australasia. (In sub-Saharan Africa, Latin America, and much of Asia, the church is vigorously promoting conversion.) Disciple-making is not evident at any scale likely to change the decades-long trend toward decline in these regions. Such an attitude also strikes me, furthermore, as importantly confused. Yes, per the oft-cited Matthew 25, following Jesus does entail compassion for the poor and otherwise marginalized. But the poor we always have with us, and we are always to do good to them. There is nothing distinctively Christian about that. Charity is a *human* imperative, part of God's general call to promote shalom. Jesus is saying that if one *doesn't* minister to the needy, one can hardly be called a serious disciple of his. Charity is just basic to being a properly functioning human being, and Jesus' mission is to guide people back to God so that we can all once more live as we ought.

The Son of God came to earth as Jesus the Messiah to right all that is wrong and to rescue all who need help, yes. The Kingdom of God is indeed a kingdom of shalom, yea and amen. So of course, Christians should be living a life that demonstrates God's values, including God's regard for the poor. That "eternal life" to which Jesus constantly refers in the Gospel according to John is indeed John's substitute for the Synoptic phrasing of "Kingdom of God/heaven" and is the *kind* of life—literally, "the life of the age to come"—we are to begin to live now under the beneficent reign of God. So, I stand with my brothers and sisters in this book who keep returning to the imperative of justice and, even more, positive *love* toward our neighbor.

Still, Jesus' parting words, his Great Commission, were not merely to live out a full-orbed life, including caring for the needy and running an uplifting worship service. Jesus specifically told his disciples on the Mount of Olives instead to fan out across the world to *make disciples*, teaching them to obey all that Jesus had commanded, in a trope reminiscent of God's original creation command to "be fruitful, multiply, fill the earth, and subdue it." Any form of Jesus-following that does not place evangelism and disciple-making front and center—as it often has been placed in many of these traditions, but not in all—walks apart from the parting word of our Lord.

Following Jesus thus occurs properly in two modes—individual and corporate—according to two vocations—making shalom and making disciples. As we have already seen, moreover, our attention is devoted to four foci: to God, to each other, to ourselves, and to the rest of the world. In terms of the creation commandment, we seek the wellbeing, the full flourishing, of God, other human beings, ourselves, and all our fellow creatures. In terms of the conversion commandment, we glorify and please God in evangelizing and then training each other toward full maturity in Christ while we also cooperate with the Spirit in pursuing our own full sanctification as well. And we bring proper attention to the gospel, Jesus said, by our good works in society and in the rest of creation. Thus, our human obeying of the creation commandment aids our Christian project of obeying the conversion commandment, even as the Christian conversion commandment is in the service of restoring humanity to God in order to fully and forever enjoy global fellowship in making shalom.

Let us now take a moment to extend our attention to congregational life. Healthy Christian communities gladly devote themselves to three sets of practices: worship of God, fellowship with each other (which ought to include Christian training, spiritually sustaining conversation, practical assistance, church discipline, and all else necessary for each other's maturing walk with the Spirit), and mission—service to the world in Jesus' name. Churches that focus too much on worship turn into spiritual spas or pep rallies. Churches that focus too much on fellowship turn into mere clubs or support groups. Churches that focus too much on mission turn into social service agencies or sales forces. No matter how different our *cultures*, all three of these *pursuits* must be thriving in any thriving church. Again, one might profitably go back over the chapters above to see whether in fact each tradition gives proper weight to all three concerns.

Further qualifications can be added to this paradigm. Time, for instance, can be a crucial consideration. Different seasons in the life of an individual or a group are rich with certain opportunities for service while discouraging to others. But perhaps we can leave this small framework here as a way of looking back over this book to see how fully articulated is each offering and in what respects this or that presentation might be bettered.

As the last discussion in this concluding essay, let us briefly consider the several ways one tradition might helpfully engage another—as an elaboration upon the initial binary of chauvinistic complacency (HH's "we have the whole truth") and self-searching attention (HH's "listening and learning").

When community A encounters community B, what community B offers community A can improve A in several different ways:

- B can augment something already in A;
- B can add something complementary to A;
- B can fulfill something in A;
- B can correct something in A; and
- B can replace something in A.

So far, so good—so long as A and B are enjoying a friendly conversation based on a similar enough epistemology that they will submit to the force of each other's arguments and readily receive improvements from each other. If such conditions cannot be met, furthermore, each conversation partner is yet free to take from the other's offerings whatever he or she can value according to his or her own lights. Each set of conversation partners thus will share a different patch of common ground, so the proceedings—the listenings and the learnings—will be necessarily ad hoc. But the blessings will be no less genuine. Muslims, Buddhists, Hindus, and Jews have benefited from such conversations across religious lines, so surely different kinds of Christians can as well. I will simply remind us that clarity as well as charity about what is and isn't possible in such encounters serves everyone well.

DIVERSITY AND BLESSING

Finally, however, we come around again to the sticky question of just how well conversations can go between people who do not share a common enough way of thinking. What then?

Christians encounter this kind of challenge all the time in any society that is not utterly their own. So why would we listen to non-Christian neighbors, and how?

We might listen so that we may learn from each other, yes, in one of the modes mentioned above.

We might listen so as to cooperate in a common concern: medical, educational, legal, and otherwise.

We might listen so as to leave each other alone in work of which we approve—what is sometimes called "comity." (Christians have experience of that on mission fields in which Presbyterians worked in one area while blessing Baptists or Anglicans working in another. Can we bless each other here at home by, say, welcoming newcomers, taking stock with them of their needs and aspirations, and eventually referring them gladly to a community across town in which they might better flourish? Jesus' new commandment in John 13 comes again to mind.)

Finally, it might be simply a matter of tolerating each other. And in the real world nowadays, mutual tolerance is no small thing—particularly when one Christian group enjoys cultural authority with the power to make it difficult for others, such as is indeed the case in Russia, parts of Africa, in China (think of the official Three-Self Church versus all others), and even in small areas such as the Dutch-Reformed-dominated village of Orange City, Iowa, where Harold Heie and I first met.

C. S. Lewis pictured "mere Christianity" as the hallway that connects the various rooms, or traditions, or communities, in God's great house. He wisely advised us that one cannot remain forever camped out in the hall but must eventually choose a room in which to reside. This book has been an exercise in enjoying extended conversation in the hall while gladly wearing the identity of one's particular room, one's own community. May we return then to our rooms determined to follow Jesus better in the way our community has found fruitful, with each branch both enriched and pruned by God through this encounter so that we may bear still more fruit in Jesus' name.

* * *

Reflections on the Essay from John Stackhouse, by Harold Heie

It is now time to ask whether the content of this book makes coherent sense to a highly regarded Christian scholar, John Stackhouse (who from now on I will refer to as "John" because of our friendship over many years).

John reflects on our ecumenical conversation in his concluding essay "Diversity and Blessing." His expressed hope is that his essay will "round out or even counterbalance the materials in the book." I believe he has accomplished both of these purposes in an admirable way.

In what follows, I will respond to highlights of John's essay that jumped out at me, concluding by addressing three concerns expressed by John, with my hope being that I will provide ideas to be discussed in ongoing conversations.

First, my heart is warmed (probably because John agrees with me and the CPs) when John states that "among the glories of Christianity is its dual emphasis on the individual and on the community." His elaboration is worth repeating: "Any version of Christianity . . . that skews toward individualism to the neglect or derogation of the Church, on the one hand, or that valorizes the Church (the congregation, or denomination, or Church as a whole) at the expense of individual dignity, responsibility, and flourishing, on the other, is substandard Christianity and warrants remedy."

I especially appreciate John's pointing out that "diversity has been a hallmark of Christianity" since the time that Jesus walked our earth, noting that "much of the Church's diversity has been simply the consequence of evangelical success. Different people, different *kinds* of people, come to Christ and bring with them all that they are." Therefore, "Diversity . . . is a mark of God's blessing as God's kingdom advances."

As a result of this legitimate diversity, John asserts, "There is no single ideal form of Christianity that somehow combines all that is good in all the others into a coherent whole," adding, "[T]his book affirms that self-contented isolation is not a sensible Christian option in the face of our own evident deficits and the resources apparently available in other communities. To become all Christ wants us to be requires us to learn from different others, not simply become more and more what we already are."

However, at the same time that John applauds diversity within the Christian Church, he also helpfully acknowledges, "Some diversity in church history has been fatally bad, manifesting in heresy and schism," with some forms of "diversity and division [having] arisen out of small- and narrow-mindedness, conceit, arrogance, intolerance, uncharity, and similar nasty traits so often warned against, already in the New Testament," where "Christians refused to accommodate each other, so preferring their own way of doing things as to split the fellowship."

So far, these reflections from John appear to me to nicely

"round out" the content of this book. But there is much room for ongoing ecumenical conversation regarding issues where John suggests a need for "counterbalance" with the content of this book. I will reflect on three such concerns.

INADEQUATE ATTENTION PAID TO EVANGELISM AND DISCIPLESHIP-MAKING: First, John expresses "some dismay at the lack of attention paid to evangelism and disciple-making in this volume," adding that he "detect[s] an occasional hint that serious Christians should 'outgrow' evangelism and serve humanity in other ways."

In defense of the CPs, their rejection of the false choice of viewing Christian living as either having a personal relationship with God or partnering with God to redeem all aspects of the creation (including unjust systemic structures) reflects their taking a both/and position.

But as in any both/and position, there is the challenge of creating a proper balance between the two poles. And John raises a legitimate concern that the CPs may not have created the best balance, placing too much emphasis on partnering with God to redeem all aspects of creation and not enough emphasis on "evangelism and disciple-making." I hope that the CPs and others will continue a conversation about that concern.

Elaborating first on John's call for more of an emphasis on evangelism, I may have contributed to such a perceived imbalance based on my experience of imbalance in the other direction—a strong emphasis on evangelism that has paid inadequate attention to Christians partnering with God to foster God's broader redemptive purposes, which include caring for the poor and marginalized in our society, one aspect of which is to seek to redeem all aspects of creation, including broken societal structures. Obviously, more conversation is needed about striking a proper balance for this both/and position.[5]

But let me close this section by reflecting on John's call for more of an emphasis on "disciple-making." Although a number of my CPs pointed to the need for "disciple-making" by suggesting that Christian traditions need to provide more instruction regarding "how to" follow Jesus by keeping his commandments, I agree with John that inadequate attention was paid to the "substance" of that instruction. My own attempt to encourage readers to think about this substance was to suggest that all Christians, in any Christian tradition, need to be encouraged to develop their own Christian ethic, which I believe is comprised of an enumeration of Christian values and beliefs about the actions that will foster the accomplishment of these values, as well as actions that will be destructive of these values.

HAROLD IS "LOOKING FOR TROUBLE" BY ENCOURAGING CONVERSATIONS ABOUT SAME-SEX MARRIAGE: A second concern that John raises is that I may be "looking for trouble" when I encourage my readers to address the issue of same-sex marriage, which "is arguably the most divisive ecclesiastical question of our time."

On the light side for a moment, John may have accurately identified the fact that "I often have more nerve than brains."

---

[5] My own take on the role that I believe evangelism should play in all Christian traditions is deeply informed by the story recorded in John 9 of Jesus restoring sight to a man who was born blind. In response to the critique of the Pharisees that Jesus was a sinner, the healed man said "I do not know if whether he is a sinner. One thing I do know, that though I was blind, now I see" (v. 25). Contrary to the manipulative, coercive means for doing evangelism that is practiced in some Christian circles, my view of "doing evangelism" at its best (based on John 9) is that "witnessing to others" should focus on telling your story about how your commitment to "accept Jesus as your Savior" has brought meaning and purpose to your life.

But, more seriously, in elaborating John suggests that my call to "listen to the stories of LGBTQ++ people" has typically not worked well, giving the example from the Anglican Diocese of New Westminster, Vancouver, where the "result of this dialogue and listening was a very public lawsuit over church property litigated before the British Columbia Supreme Court that prompted a very public schism."

John reports that this schism emerged despite the fact that "under the direction of a determined bishop, the diocese undertook listening and group study and public discussion for over a decade," and this listening "included attention to the poignant testimonies of people identifying themselves with gender and sexual minorities, testimonies offered by those people themselves as well as by others on their behalf, in large groups and small." John regretfully concludes that "Listening hasn't seemed to help," asking the compelling question, "Why not?"

My initial response to John's "Why Not?" question, that I will elaborate on in my concluding essay, is that in the disastrous example he gives from Vancouver, there may have been inadequate attention given to a proper "methodology" for orchestrating a loving and respectful conversation about such a "hot-button" issue. As a counterexample to the Vancouver example, I refer the reader to the Conversation I hosted on my website on "human sexuality" (which can be accessed by going to the "Previous" icon on the top of my Home Page). If you read through the postings for that conversation, I believe you will agree that the CPs managed to carry out a "loving and respectful" conversation, primarily because they agreed up-front to a set of stipulated "Guidelines for Respectful Conversation.[6] Again, I will say more about that "methodology" in my concluding essay.

[6] My report on this conversation is contained in my book *Respectful LGBT Conversations: Seeking Truth, Giving Love, and Modeling Christian Unity*. Eugene, OR: Cascade Books, 2018.

A Major Reason Why Harold's Call for Respectful Conversations Will Not Work: This is John's most pressing concern. In strong language, he asserts that there is an "intrinsic and inescapable problem" that is "a major reason why the kind of conversation that HH [that is me] desires simply cannot, and does not take place." That intractable problem is that there exist three "incommensurate styles of theology." John labels these three incommensurate styles "liberal," "evangelical," and "conservative."

Not being a theologian or biblical scholar, I am not competent to evaluate John's argument that it is the existence of these three incommensurate styles of doing theology that causes just listening to be inadequate. It is my hope that many of the CPs, most of whom are theologians or biblical scholars, will continue a conversation about the efficacy, or not, of theologians just listening to one another.

However, allow me one brief reflection, as an amateur, drawing on my experiences over the past dozen years, in trying to orchestrate respectful conversations among Christians having some strong disagreements. First, I believe that a careful reading of this book will reveal that some highly regarded theologians have found some common ground, without putting themselves in a liberal, conservative, or evangelical box, by practicing what I have called "strong listening" in contrast to the much more common "weak listening." I will say more about the nature of such "strong listening" when I propose a "methodology" for orchestrating loving and respectful conversations about contentious issues in my concluding essay.

Conclusion: What I Have Learned from Our Conversation

Harold Heie

The narrative you have just read is replete with statements pointing to what twelve CPs have learned from one another. In this concluding essay, I will first enumerate the primary "beliefs" I now embrace about what it means to follow Jesus, which will include many new insights that I gleaned from the postings of the CPs and some beliefs that I have held in rudimentary form before our conversation, the truth of which were reinforced by comments from the CPs.

I will then reflect on the "process" that was used in this ecumenical conversation to sort through the agreements and disagreements that our CPs had about what it means to follow Jesus, including a proposed "methodology" for orchestrating future conversations about contentious issues that I believe will prove to be loving and respectful.

These "Truths" I Now Embrace

#1: I should avail myself of the resources for spiritual

growth (i.e., rituals for worship and practice of the sacraments) provided in the Christian tradition in which I worship at the same time that I take concrete actions in response to the commandments of Jesus, especially his commandment, recorded in Matthew 25, that I minister to the needs of the poor, persecuted, and marginalized in our society. It is both/and, not either/or.

#2: There is much room for freedom and spontaneity in deciding how to follow Jesus, but that freedom has "boundaries." I should formulate a Christian ethic that starts with my understanding of Christian values, on the basis of which I should make daily decisions that promote the realization of these values and avoid actions that are destructive of these values.

#3. To faithfully follow Jesus is a dynamic process that I pursue without having all the answers to contentious questions due to my finitude and fallibility. It is in the process of following Jesus that I discern better answers and gain greater insight into how I should continue to follow Jesus.

#4: "Who I am" deeply informs my decisions on how I should follow Jesus. This includes my particularities, such as my gender, my race and ethnicity, my socio-economic status, and my sexual orientation, as well as my biography (my personal story) and even my personality.

#5: Because no two Christians are identical in their particularities and biographies, a Christian from another tradition, or my own tradition, who disagrees with me may see things that I miss because of "who

CONCLUSION

he/she is," and I may see things that he/she misses because of "who I am." Therefore, my conversation with such a person should start with attempts to understand the beliefs of the other person and the reasons we have for our differing beliefs.

#6. Regarding "salvation," God wishes to save individual persons from self-centeredness; calling them to lovingly care for others, especially the poor and marginalized in society. But the "good news of the gospel" is even broader, since God wishes to redeem all aspects of Creation, including systemic structures like the political realm, and I should seek to "partner with God," contributing to God's redemptive work in ways that best fit with my giftedness.

#7. It is a false choice to view my Christian commitment as focusing on "Jesus and me" *or* contributing to God's redemption of the world. It is both/and, not either/or.

#8: The task to which Christians are committed must include a social and political vision that calls for communal action, not just individual action.

#9: I need to be wary of the possibility of my Christian tradition deteriorating from a heartfelt renewal movement to a lifeless, moribund tradition. This requires my being open to the possible emergence of new leaders in my tradition who will become "this generation's reforming fires."

#10: In responding to the calling of Jesus recorded in Matthew 25 to work for justice for the marginalized members of our society, such as racial groups who have been discriminated against since the founding of America, I must put myself in situations that take me beyond understanding the causes of the pain experienced by these marginalized groups to actually feeling their pain.

#11: A good starting place for me to follow Jesus is for me to regularly search Scriptures, always striving for a better understanding of truth; for me to regularly pray to God, offering up my petitions and my gratitude for God's grace; for me to love and serve others as Jesus did; and for me to fully live out my Christian faith in community with other members of the body of Christ.

#12: I should avoid the conceit of thinking "it is my way or the highway." I should not make my Christian experience normative by believing that other Christians, within and beyond my tradition, need to follow Jesus my way. There exists a rich multiplicity of ways to follow Jesus that reflects each person's uniqueness.

#13: I should expose myself to what Christian traditions other than my own believe about what it means to follow Jesus in order to gain insights to inform my aspiration to faithfully follow Jesus.

A Proposed "Methodology" for Orchestrating Loving and Respectful Conversations About Contentious Issues

I recommend two prior agenda items for a FIRST session: starting that session by making clear the purpose of the conversation and then focusing on getting to "know one another" by discussing two non-threatening questions.

CONCLUSION

It should be made clear that the purpose of the conversation is NOT to win an argument. Rather the purpose is to seek to find some common ground based on gaining an adequate understanding of the positions taken by all the CPs and the reasons they have for holding those positions.

The remainder of the first session should then be devoted to addressing the following two non-threatening questions:

- What elements of your personal story make this an important topic for you?
- What do you hope to get out of this conversation?

After the CPs have gotten to know each other better by means of this non-threatening first session, I recommend that the SECOND session be devoted to a discussion of the following "Guidelines for Respectful Conversation."

- I will try to listen well, providing each person with a welcoming space to express her perspective on the issue at hand.
- I will seek to empathetically understand the reasons another person has for her perspective.
- I will express my perspective and my reasons for holding that perspective with clarity and conviction, but with a non-coercive style that invites conversation with a person who disagrees with me.
- In my conversation with a person who disagrees with me, I will explore whether we can find some common ground by critically examining my own view in light of her contrary view and the reasons she has for her view.
- Guided by the underlying values of humility, cour-

age, patience, and love, when we cannot find common ground, I will always engage the person who disagrees with me in a way that demonstrates respect and concern for her well-being and does not foreclose the possibility of future conversations.

The fourth guideline above calls for what I call "strong listening", which goes beyond being polite, which is the "weak listening" that is characterized by an agreement to not interrupt a person who disagrees with you. The shortcoming of such "weak listening" is that while not interrupting the other, you may only be thinking of what you will say when you get your turn to speak. Strong listening requires that you critically examine your beliefs in light of what you hear the other person saying.

As I suggested in my response to John Stackhouse, this second recommendation emerges from my belief that that the online conversation I hosted on my website on the very contentious issue of human sexuality, including same-sex marriage, proved to be loving and respectful because I made it clear that the CPs were invited to attend the subsequent sessions ONLY IF they agreed to abide by these "Guidelines for Respectful Conversation."

After these two initial foundational sessions, The CPs who have agreed to abide by these guidelines for ongoing conversation will be adequately prepared to "jump into the fray" by beginning to lay bare their disagreements in subsequent sessions. But there is a good way and a bad way to do that.

The bad way is to quickly enable any CP to tell other CPs why he (or she) is right and they are wrong. That will just bring about defensiveness. Rather, as suggested by Richard Mouw, president emeritus of Fuller Theological Seminary in Pasadena (CA), who has graciously written the foreword to this book, a better opening gambit for addressing a CP who

CONCLUSION

you know disagrees with you is to make the following request:

Please help me to better understand your position on this issue and the reasons you have for holding to your position.

Mouw's experience, in the numerous dialogues about interfaith issues in which he has participated, is that such an opening request may well lead to "reciprocity" (WOW! Richard really wants to know what I believe and the reasons I have for my belief. Maybe I should do likewise).

At its best, my focus on adequately understanding the other and critically examining your own beliefs in light of that understanding requires that you not be so enamored with your own beliefs that you fail to grasp the richness in what you hear as you carefully listen to the other person.

My experience suggests that if you are willing to adopt the methodological recommendations outlined above, you will be able to orchestrate a loving and respectful conversation about any contentious issue, including human sexuality.

About the Authors

HAROLD HEIE served as Founding Director of the Center for Christian Studies (now the Center for Faith & Inquiry) at Gordon College and as Vice President for Academic Affairs at Messiah College and Northwestern College in Iowa, after teaching mathematics at Gordon College and The King's College. He holds a PhD in aerospace sciences from Princeton University and served as a trustee of the Center for Public Justice, as a Senior Fellow at the Council for Christian Colleges and Universities (CCCU), and as a Senior Fellow at The Colossian Forum. He has also served as a co-director of CASA of Sioux County (Center for Assistance, Service and Advocacy), a non-profit devoted to welcoming, empowering, and celebrating people from all cultures, with a special focus on helping his new Latino neighbors to flourish.

In 2011, Heie founded the Respectful Conversation Project on his website, respectfulconversation.net, which is devoted to encouraging and modeling respectful conversations concerning contentious issues about which Christians have strong disagreements. His website has hosted four major electronic conversations (eCircles), the highlights of which have been reported in the following four books: *Evangelicals on Public Policy Issues: Sustaining a Respectful Political Conversation* (2014); *A Future for American Evangelicalism: Commitment, Openness, and Conversation* (2015); *Respectful LGBT Conversations: Seeking Truth, Giving Love, and Modeling Christian Unity* (2018); and *Reforming American Politics: A Christian Perspective on Moving Past Conflict to Conversation* (2019).

JOHN G. STACKHOUSE JR. has enjoyed preaching in a wide array of churches, from Lutheran to Pentecostal to Mennonite to Presbyterian. He currently teaches at a Baptist university while worshiping with Anglicans and writing regularly for *Faith Today*, Canada's national evangelical magazine.

A graduate of both evangelical (Wheaton College) and liberal (University of Chicago) schools of theology, he has given guest lectures at religious schools as varied as Pepperdine University, Yale Divinity School, Brigham Young University, Calvin Theological Seminary, New College, Edinburgh, and Moody Bible Institute.

Stackhouse's journalism has shown up in Christian periodicals as disparate as *The Christian Century*, *Christianity Today*, *The Reformed Journal*, *Books & Culture*, and *Geez*, and he currently serves on the editorial board of *The Anglican Journal* in Canada.

Author and editor of over a dozen books, he has applied his scholarship to church history, theology, ethics, and philosophy of religion, with his three most recent books reflecting that range: *Why You're Here: Ethics for the Real World*, *Can I Believe? Christianity for the Hesitant*, and *Evangelicalism: A Very Short Introduction* (all from Oxford).

ABOUT THE AUTHORS

RICHARD J. MOUW earned his PhD in Philosophy from the University of Chicago, and after teaching at Calvin College (now Calvin University) for seventeen years he moved to the faculty of Fuller Theological Seminary in 1985. In 1993 he was appointed as Fuller's president and served in that role for twenty years. During that time, he also served as the president of the Association of Theological Schools.

Mouw has been actively engaged in interfaith dialogues, particularly with Mormons, Jews, and Muslims. He also co-chaired with a Catholic bishop the official Reformed-Catholic Dialogue, engaging in a five-year joint study of the sacraments.

Mouw is presently the Senior Research Fellow at the Paul B. Henry Institute for Faith and Politics at Calvin University. His most recent book, published by InterVarsity Press, is *How to be a Patriotic Christian*.

Contributors

The following twelve contributors are presented in chronological order, according to the generally agreed-upon date of origination of the traditions they represent, starting with the oldest tradition.

Orthodox: David Ford is Professor of Church History at St. Tikhon's Orthodox Theological Seminary. He earned a Bachelor of Arts degree in History from Colgate University; a Master of Divinity degree from Oral Roberts University; and a PhD from Drew University.

David has published six books, including *Marriage as a Path to Holiness: Lives of Married Saints* (co-authored with his wife Dr. Mary Ford) (1994); *Women and Men in the Early Church: The Vision of Saint John Chrysostom* (1996); *Wisdom for Today from the Early Church* (2014); and *Saint Tikhon of Moscow: Instructions and Teachings for the American Orthodox Faithful (1898–1907)* (2016). He has also written numerous journal articles, including "St. Macarios of Egypt and John Wesley: Variations on the Theme of Sanctification" in the *Greek Orthodox Theological Review*; "The Interrelationship of Clergy and Laity within the Family of God according to Saint John Chrysostom" in *St. Vladimir's Theological Quarterly*; "2000 Years of Church History as Seen through the Lives of Some of the Most Significant Saints of Each Century" in the *Tikhonaire*. Dr. Ford has also published encyclopedia articles on "St. John Chrysostom" in *The Concise Encyclopedia of Preaching*, and "History of Orthodoxy" in *The HarperCollins Encyclopedia of Religion in Canada*. He also, along with Dr. Mary and Fr. Theodore Petrides, wrote and edited the 21 one-page thematic articles in the Old Testament portion of the complete Orthodox Study Bible, published in 2008.

ROMAN CATHOLIC: Christina Wassell is a convert to Roman Catholicism striving to live the Good Life in the woods of central Massachusetts by fostering a "Domestic Church" that has two dimensions that seek to build "Catholic Culture." The first dimension focuses on her family and home. Christina and her husband, Scott, built a little homestead with their own hands in 2010. Her vocation of "building home" includes growing a garden, raising (and slaughtering!) animals for meat and eggs, educating her seven boys at home, and living out days rooted in the seasons of the Liturgical Calendar to dictate times of fasting and feasting, prayer and penance. The Holy Family's "hidden life at Nazareth" serves as inspiration for this life centered on the home and family.

The second dimension of the Domestic Church that Christina seeks to model focuses on the importance of community. For Christina and her family, the drive to build Catholic Culture must obviously involve real intentionality about their wider community. For the last decade the Wassells have worked with families in their church and others to build a robust experience of "real life" for themselves and their children. This life includes singing and playing music together, hosting a yearly theater camp for 40+ homeschoolers, learning to contra dance and swing dance and organizing regular dances for young people, and assembling all manner of book groups and classes for young learners, and praying together. This life is full of cooking together, eating together, celebrating the feasts together, and praying together.

The Wassell family enjoyed a winding path through Protestantism before becoming Catholic. They worshiped at broadly Evangelical and Methodist churches before attending a high-church Episcopal congregation, which had strong devotion to both the Bible and liturgy. This ultimately set the Wassells on the path to Rome. Their coming into the Roman Catholic church in 2010 was followed up by a more recent move to attending the Latin Mass. The Wassells are now thriving at an FSSP parish in Providence, Rhode Island, and feel that for the first time they are enjoying the real fullness of the ancient roots of Roman Catholicism.

Christina is a graduate of Gordon College, with a BA in English. She has been teaching in a professional capacity since 2005 at New Hope Courses for Homeschoolers in Boxford, Massachusetts. This includes teaching literature and writing and ancient and Medieval history to middle schoolers, as well as creative writing workshops for younger students.

LUTHERAN: Mark Ellingsen is a Lutheran (ELCA) pastor who has served for nearly three decades on the faculty of the largest Historic Black seminary in the US, the Interdenominational Theological Center in Atlanta. Prior to assuming that position he served as a parish pastor, served on the faculty of a Lutheran Seminary, and spent six years in international ecumenism on the staff of the Institute for Ecumenical Research headquartered in Strasbourg, France.

Raised bi-culturally by Norwegian immigrant parents, Mark has a Yale PhD and is the author of 24 books (two more are presently being published) and over 400 published articles. His most recent books are a textbook for Intro to Theology courses titled *Theological Formation: Making Theology Your Own* (Mercer University Press), a book on how to cope with the challenges of globalization and internet connectivity titled *Finding Peaks and Valleys in a Flat World* (Vernon Press), and a book explaining the growth of the Nones (religiously unaffiliated) and what to do about these developments titled *Ever Hear of Feuerbach? That's Why American and European Christianity Are in Such a Funk!* (Cascade Books). A proud Confessional Lutheran (he loves Luther), Mark is also a raving "ecumeniac," as most of his education and the academic positions he has held have been in ecumenical institutions.

ANABAPTIST: **Michael King**, Telford, Pennsylvania, has long been an editor and publisher, first through Herald Press (Scottdale, PA, 1989-97) and then more recently as owner and publisher since 1997 at Cascadia Publishing House LLC (Telford, PA). He has been dean at Eastern Mennonite Seminary and Vice President at Eastern Mennonite University (2010-17) and during that period was also dean at the EMU Graduate and Professional School (2016-17). He has been pastor in diverse congregational settings, ranging from Germantown Mennonite Church (Philadelphia, PA, 1982-89) to Spring Mount (PA) Mennonite Church (1997-2008).

As author and publisher, King has addressed theology and culture, including implications of postmodernity and the "emerging church" movement. King is co-editor (with Harold Heie) of *Mutual Treasure: Seeking Better Ways for Christians and Culture to Converse* (Cascadia, 2009), editor of *Stumbling Toward*

CONTRIBUTORS

a Genuine Conversation on Homosexuality (Cascadia, 2007), and co-editor of Anabaptist Preaching: A Conversation Between Pulpit, Pew, and Bible (Cascadia, 2004). He is the author of Trackless Wastes and Stars to Steer By: Christian Identity in a Homeless Age (Herald, 1990); Fractured Dance: Gadamer and Mennonite Conversation On Homosexuality, C. Henry Smith series, vol. 3 (Pandora U.S., 2001); and many articles in a wide variety of magazines and journals, including Christian Century. He is co-author (with Ron Sider) of Preaching about Life in a Threatening World (Westminster, 1987).

ANGLICAN: **Randall Balmer** is a prize-winning historian and Emmy Award nominee. He earned a PhD from Princeton University in 1985 and taught as Professor of American Religious History at Columbia University for 27 years before becoming the Mandel Family Professor of Arts and Sciences at Dartmouth College in 2012. He has been a visiting professor at Princeton, Yale, Northwestern, and Emory universities and in the Columbia University Graduate School of Journalism. He was a visiting professor at Yale Divinity School from 2004 to 2008.

Dr. Balmer has published widely in both scholarly journals and in the popular press. His op-ed articles have appeared in newspapers across the country, including the Los Angeles Times, the Des Moines Register, the Philadelphia Inquirer, the Dallas Morning News, the St. Louis Post-Dispatch, the Hartford Courant, the Minneapolis Star-Tribune, the Anchorage Daily News, and the New York Times. His work has also appeared in the New Republic, the New York Times Book Review, Christian Century, the Nation, the Chronicle of Higher Education, and Washington Post Book World. Dr. Balmer is regularly asked to comment on religion in American life, and he has appeared frequently on network television, on NPR, and on both the Colbert Report and the *Daily Show, with John Stewart*. He has been an expert witness in several First Amendment cases, including *Snyder v. Phelps* and *Glassroth v. Moore*, the so-called Alabama Ten Commandments case. Dr. Balmer has published more than a dozen books, including *God in the White House: How Faith Shaped the Presidency from John F. Kennedy to George W. Bush* and *The Making of Evangelicalism: From Revivalism to Politics and Beyond*. His second book, *Mine Eyes Have Seen the Glory: A Journey into the Evangelical Subculture in America*, now in its fourth edition, was made into an award-winning, three-part documentary for PBS. Dr. Balmer wrote and hosted that series as well as a two-part series on creationism and a documentary on Billy Graham. He has lectured around the country in such venues as the Commonwealth Club of California and the Chautauqua Institution and, under the auspices of the State Department, in Austria and Lebanon.

REFORMED: Wesley Granberg-Michaelson served as General Secretary of the Reformed Church in America for 17 years, from 1994–2011. He is a graduate of Hope College and Western Theological Seminary. Earlier in his career he served as the Legislative Assistant to US Senator Mark O. Hatfield, and then as the Associate Editor of *Sojourners* magazine when it was founded. He played a leading role in establishing Christian Churches Together in the USA, and is known globally for his ecumenical leadership, including service as Director of Church and Society for the World Council of Churches. Presently he serves on the boards of Sojourners, Church Innovations, and the Global Christian Forum. His most recent book is *Without Oars: Casting Off into a Life of Pilgrimage*. While serving as a Kluge Fellow at the Library of Congress, he wrote *From Times Square to Timbuktu: The Post Christian West Meets the Non-Western Church*. Among his other books are *Future Faith: Ten Challenges Reshaping Christianity in the 21st Century* (2018) and a memoir, *Unexpected Destinations: An Evangelical Pilgrim-*

CONTRIBUTORS

age to World Christianity. He has been awarded two honorary doctorate degrees. Wes's speaking and continuing work with the global church has taken him to all corners of the world.

BAPTIST: **David Gushee** (PhD, Union Theological Seminary, New York) is Distinguished University Professor of Christian Ethics at Mercer University and Chair of Christian Social Ethics at Vrije Universiteit ("Free University") Amsterdam/IBTS.

Dr. Gushee is the elected past-president of both the American Academy of Religion and Society of Christian Ethics, signaling his role as one of the world's leading Christian scholars. He is author, coauthor, editor, or coeditor of more than 25 books and over 175 academic book chapters, journal articles, and reviews. His most recognized works include *Righteous Gentiles of the Holocaust, Kingdom Ethics, The Sacredness of Human Life,* and *Changing Our Mind.* His new book, *After Evangelicalism,* charts a theological and ethical course for post-evangelical Christians, a course he more personally relates in his memoir, *Still Christian.* All together his books have sold over 100,000 copies and been translated into a dozen languages. Over a full 28-year career, he's been a devoted teacher and mentor as to college students, seminarians, and PhD students. He's also led significant activist efforts on climate, torture, and LGBTQ++ inclusion.

For the general media, Dr. Gushee has written hundreds of opinion pieces and given interviews to scores of major outlets and podcasts. Along with his friend Jeremy Hall, he also co-hosts a popular podcast called "Kingdom Ethics."

PIETIST: **Christopher Gehrz** (PhD, Yale) is professor of history at Bethel University in St. Paul, Minnesota, where he teaches courses on modern European military/diplomatic, sports, and religious history and has previously served as department chair and faculty president.

Chris recently wrote a religious biography of aviator Charles Lindbergh and co-edited a devotional featuring forty Christian historians. But most of his publications concern the Christian tradition known as Pietism, with books including *The Pietist Option: Hope for the Renewal of Christianity* (IVP Academic, 2017) and *The Pietist Vision of Christian Higher Education: Forming Whole and Holy Persons* (IVP Academic, 2015). He also blogs regularly at *The Pietist Schoolman* and the Patheos group blog *The Anxious Bench*.

WESLEYAN: **Sarah Lancaster** is Professor of Theology at Methodist Theological School in Ohio. She is the author of *Pursuit of Happiness: Blessing and Fulfillment in Christian Faith* (Eugene, OR: Wipf and Stock, 2010), which is a study of John Wesley's understanding of holiness and happiness as the goal of Christian life. She has also published a number of articles and essays on John Wesley's theology and has served in leadership positions, such as co-chair of the Wesleyan Studies Group of the American Academy of Religion and North America and co-chair of the Oxford Institute of Methodist Theological Studies. She has served The United Methodist Church in several ecumenical dialogues, including working as co-moderator in the production of *The Church: Towards a Common Vision* by the Faith and Order Commission of the World Council of Churches.

THE BLACK CHURCH: **Farris Blount** is a PhD candidate at Boston University School of Theology studying practical theology. His research interests lie at the intersection of church and society as he seeks to explore how we can build communities of care, concern, and human flourishing in the midst of rampant individualism, within Christian church contexts and Black church spaces in particular. Farris aims to apply an interdisciplinary lens to his work, relying on theological,

CONTRIBUTORS

sociological, and qualitative research methods to examine the impacts of race, class, and gender within ecclesial spaces.

LATTER-DAY SAINTS: Robert Millet is Professor Emeritus of Religious Education at Brigham Young University. He received bachelors and masters degrees in psychology from BYU (1971, 1973) and his PhD in Religious Studies from Florida State University (1983). After joining the BYU religion faculty in 1983, he served as chair of the Department of Ancient Scripture, dean of the College of Religious Education, and Richard L. Evans Professor of Religious Understanding. He retired from teaching at BYU in January 2014.

Since 1990, Professor Millet has been engaged in interfaith relations. In May of 2000 he and Richard J. Mouw, at the time President of Fuller Theological Seminary, provided leadership for an academic dialogue between six Evangelical scholars and six Latter-day Saint scholars. That dialogue has continued for over 20 years. Dr. Millet has also been involved in academic dialogues with scholars from the Church of the Nazarene, Community of Christ (formerly the Reorganized Church of Jesus Christ of Latter-day Saints), and a dialogue with seven Christian scholars, sponsored by the John A. Widtsoe Foundation at the University of Southern California. Over the years, the dialogues have centered primarily on theological topics or denominational insights into selected New Testament passages.

Millet is the author or editor of many books and articles, dealing mostly with the doctrine and history of The Church of Jesus Christ of Latter-day Saints and its relationship to other faiths. Books that reflect his interfaith involvement include *A Different Jesus? The Christ of the Latter-day Saints* (Eerdmans, 2005); *Salvation in Christ: Comparative Christian Views* (BYU Religious Studies Center, 2005); *Claiming Christ: A Mormon-Evangelical Debate* (Baker Books, 2007), co-authored with

Gerald R. McDermott; *By What Authority? The Vital Question of Religious Authority in Christianity* (Mercer, 2010); *Talking Doctrine: Mormons and Evangelicals in Conversation* (InterVarsity Press, 2015); and, *Life Beyond the Grave: Christian Interfaith Perspectives* (BYU Religious Studies Center, 2019).

PENTECOSTAL: J. Terry Todd has served for more than two decades on the Theological School faculty at Drew University, where he teaches the history of Christianity, pastoral formation, and worship and liturgy. He holds a BA from Boston University, an MDiv from Harvard Divinity School, and a PhD from Columbia University, and is the author of many articles on religious life in US contexts. His academic and ministry work involves assembling a toolkit of ritual experience that blends Methobapticostal worship styles with contemplative spirituality. Terry is committed to a ministry that is anti-racist, nurturing to all bodies and souls, forward thinking, and relevant, yet bringing whatsoever is good, kind, and beautiful from all Christian traditions. Terry holds ministerial standing in the United Church of Christ. He serves on the Educational Council of the Fellowship of Affirming Ministries (TFAM) and has served on the advisory committee of TFAM Global. Terry is also an associate pastor at Rivers of Living Water UCC in New York City, where he is a part of a Pentecostal community of radical joy and hope.

www.ingramcontent.com/pod-product-compliance
Lightning Source LLC
Chambersburg PA
CBHW050556170426
43201CB00011B/1716